D1509918

FROM THE BEGINNING

A First Reader In American History

Text by Judith Bailey

Edited by and Procedures by Joan Ashkenas

JAG PUBLICATIONS

★ ★ ★ ★ ★ ★ ★ ★ ★ ★ ★ ★ ★ ★ ★ ★ ★ ★ ★

Acknowledgments

It is a great pleasure to acknowledge our deepest gratitude to the following people:

To Steven Sloan, of the Los Angeles Unified School District's Secondary Bilingual Education Department, for his scholarly reading of individual chapters, for his time and his interest.

To Dr. Leonard Pitt, historian, of California State University, Northridge, for his excellent suggestions and criticisms after reading this manuscript.

To Lefty Fontenrose, whose maps are evidence of his artistry and high standards.

To the librarians at University of California at Los Angeles, Special Collections Department, and to Marilyn Wandrus, of Washington D.C., diligent researcher in the National Archives and Library of Congress, whose invaluable assistance brought forth most of the illustrations for this volume.

To Robert L. Goldfarb, whose literary skills and reading of the manuscript left few pages unimproved.

Published by JAG Publications
11288 Ventura Boulevard
Studio City, California 91604
Telephone: (818) 505-9002
Web site: www.jagpublications-esl.com

Cover photograph "Liberty Enlightening the World" courtesy Library of Congress

Design by Words & Deeds, San Jose

Printed in the United States of America

Library of Congress Catalog Card Number 90-91526
ISBN 0-943327-07-5

Revised Fifth Edition 1998
10 9 8 7 6 5

Contents

List of Illustrations

GREENLAND

RUSSIA

ALASKA

CANADA

UNITED STATES

Atlantic
Ocean

MEX.

Hawaii

Cuba
Belz.
Jam.
DRep.
Haiti

Guy.
Sur.
FrG.

Guat.
ESal.
Hon.
Nic.
CR
Pan.

Ven.

Col.

Ecu.

SOUTH
AMERICA

Pacific Ocean

Peru

Bol.

Brazil

Par.

Uru.

Chile

Arg.

NEW
ZEALAND

Falk. Isls.

The WORLD

ANTARCTICA

To the Instructor

From The Beginning presents American history in broad terms. Our major intent is to put within reach of as many students as possible a good and general acquaintance with this subject. While the book is designed as a general reader, it also presents personalities, dramatic events, and controversial issues of each period.

The chronological format can facilitate its use with other survey textbooks, but it stands on its own, as well. Overviews beginning each chapter provide continuity. Direction is provided by Reading Comprehension questions that encourage thoughtful response.

We have tried to keep the language uncomplicated in order to offer students the opportunity to read American history with both enjoyment and relative ease. It is our hope that this volume will instill in students an eagerness to pursue American history in more detail as their reading skills improve.

To a large extent *From The Beginning* requires dictionary work of the student. Ability to use the dictionary is very basic to literacy. Because some students may have arrived at the intermediate level without that skill, a dictionary lesson which has been widely tested is included. It can also be found in our publication of short stories, *Begin In English*, which might be considered a primer for this history text. In both, the language is comparatively simple. But here, the length of chapters, the concepts and the necessary vocabulary raise this text to the next higher reading level.

Many times during their reading, students can guess the meaning of a new word through context without using the dictionary. Often they don't need to know the exact meaning of a word, or look it up, because the general idea is clear. It is preferable, in this case, for the student's train of thought not to be broken by going to the dictionary. However, there are other times when consulting a dictionary will be necessary.

You will find that some of the vocabulary has been introduced through definitions appearing immediately after a word. For example, Chapter 1, Story 1, on Columbus contains a sentence with these words: "a sure way to get them, he believes, is to discover a sea route, a way by sea." All through the book, other words students may not know are numbered and defined in the section where they first appear. The definitions for these are always in the context of the story. For example, in the Overview, Chapter 1, page 2, the word "preserve" is defined: to keep fresh and good. But in the dictionary you will find another meaning: to prepare food, as by canning or by salting. Many words will have more than one definition, of course. Students may require assistance to use the definition in the correct context. Obviously, using the dictionary is as important to their understanding the content as to increasing their vocabularies.

★ ★

Again as in *Begin In English*, we have controlled vocabulary as much as possible. We are guided here, too, by the fundamental list, *The 2,000 Most Frequently Used Words In English*, edited by Robert J. Dixson. In this resource, the first 500 words follow the Thorndike-Lorge list. The second 500 were derived, with some modification, mainly from the *Interim Report On Vocabulary Selection For Teaching English As A Foreign Language* (Palmer, Thorndike, West, Sapir, etc.). The remaining 1,000 words of this list were compiled from Thorndike, emphasizing assessed needs for teaching conversation in English to primary level students. Of necessity, there is much vocabulary here that is outside that list. Words not found in the list are defined in each section as described above.

We have tried to convey the sense of each period through illustrations, most of which are of their own time. The maps are new and easy to read.

We have not shied away from some of America's most controversial episodes. Ideally, a reader should keep an open mind while developing a healthy skepticism. There are oppressors and victims, and sometimes the lines between them are not clear. Just reading American history should give one an appreciation of the complexities of government in a dynamic country of such diversity.

A complete bibliography is available upon request.

There are many useful texts available as references for general American history. For your consideration we can name three which are quite comprehensive:

Rise of the American Nation: Liberty Edition, Combined, 1982, Harcourt Brace;

American Pageant: A History of the Republic, 2 volumes, 7th Edition Thomas A. Bailey and David M. Kennedy, 1983, Heath;

The American People: Creating a Nation and a Society, Second Edition Combined, Gary B. Nash and Julie Roy Jeffrey, 1990, Harper & Row.

Joan Ashkenas, Editor
1990

To the Student

In this book you are going to read about some of America's greatest events and people. This story moves fast. It will help you in a general way to understand America as it is today. As you read, may things are going to surprise you, or make you sad or angry. Others will make you smile.

Over many thousands of years, different people from many different countries come to America. But the history of the United States of America as a nation begins only about 200 years ago. You are going to understand why people travel so far to look for a better life for themselves.

No country has a perfect history, where only good things happen. But you will see why people have always come to the United States, and why they stay, even when conditions are very difficult. You will understand how people of good will can make good things happen in a free country.

Learning to Use the Dictionary

A. **Alphabetizing.** Use the alphabet to help you do the following exercises.

a b c d e f g h i j k l m n o p q r s t u v w x y z

1. Put these letters in correct order:

b c a _____ _____ _____

i g h _____ _____ _____

o m n _____ _____ _____

2. Put these words in correct order according to their first letters:

sit baby light house _____ _____ _____ _____

fast apple cake down _____ _____ _____ _____

3. These words have the same first letter. Arrange them according to their second letters:

buy big boy _____ _____ _____

pin pan put pet _____ _____ _____ _____

shell sell spell _____ _____ _____

4. These words begin with the same two letters. Put them in order according to their third letters:

plan plum plot _____ _____ _____ _____

flock flake flute _____ _____ _____ _____

street stamp stop _____ _____ _____ _____

through thought thin _____ _____ _____ _____

B. **Using the Dictionary**

Open the dictionary to where the letter 'b' begins. Notice that the first words you see following the 'b' all have 'a' for their second letter. Now look at their third letter.

Notice that these third letters follow in alphabetical order: first 'a', then 'b', then 'c', through the rest of the alphabet. Using this idea, let's practice and look up the following words: baby, back, bad, bag.

Now turn the pages and pass the letters 'ba' until you find words beginning with 'be.' Look up these words: beach, bed, before, begin.

Now continue turning pages until you find words starting with 'bi.' Find these words: bicycle, big, bill, bird.

Now look for these words: black, boat, brake, bud.

C.   Dictionary Work

Open the dictionary and look at the top of any page. You can see two words in dark letters. The word on the left gives you the first word on the page. The word on the right gives you the last word on the page, and between these, all words are in alphabetical order, according to their second, third, fourth, etc. letters.

Let's practice finding some words. Turn to the letter 'b' and look for the word 'bad.' You know it is close to the beginning of the 'b' because its second letter is 'a.' It comes after words beginning with 'bab' and 'bac' because 'b' and 'c' come before 'd' in the alphabet.

Let's try another word. Turn to the letter 'n' and find the word 'not.' The second letter, 'o', of 'not' is more towards the middle of the alphabet, so you must pass up words beginning with 'na', 'ne', 'ni', and find words beginning with 'no.' Now you need to find the third letter, 't', after the 'o.' Look for it in its alphabetical order at the top of the pages.

Before the Beginning
The First Americans

Thirty thousand years ago, maybe even more, people start to come, or migrate, to the Americas from Siberia. These first Americans leave no written history of their great migration. But we are learning much about them because modern scientists are finding their stone hunting tools, the charcoal of their cooking fires, and some human bones. Scientific tests show exactly how old these things are.

Scientists believe that these people are Asians. During the time of their migrations, a large part of the world is covered by the glaciers of the last Ice Age. Food is hard to find in frozen Siberia. For this reason, some of the hunters who live there begin to move east and south, looking for better hunting.

Today, fifty-six miles of water and islands, the Bering Strait, separate Alaska from Siberia. But in the Ice Age, which lasts until about twelve thousand years ago, the water levels of the oceans are lower. Water in the Bering Strait is so low that Alaska and Siberia are connected by a land bridge. Across this bridge walk groups of The People, as we think they call themselves. They keep coming for thousands of years from the Old World. As they enter Alaska, they are discovering the New World.

At that time, parts of Alaska are warmer than now. The land is rich with tall grass, trees, rivers, and lakes. There are mammoths (early elephants), camels, wolves, lions, and bison, many of them larger than they are today. And there is a kind of small horse that disappears from America when the Ice Age ends. Horses are not seen again until the Spanish explorers bring them in the fifteenth century.

The People, whom Europeans later mistakenly call "Indians," gradually migrate across North and Central America and down into South America. Whether they are originally one people or several peoples we still do not know. As centuries pass, large groups separate from each other. Differences in appearance, language and culture, the way that they live, become very great.

Some of The People continue to hunt big animals with their stone spears. Later, as the ice melts and the land warms, they begin to farm. The first Americans grow corn, squash, potatoes, pumpkin, pineapple, tomatoes. These, and many other foods, are not known in the rest of the world until the explorers of the fifteenth and sixteenth centuries return home with them. The People who settle near the oceans and rivers become fishermen. Those who make their home in what is now the Southwestern United States build apartment house villages which we call pueblos. The most famous of these is five stories tall and has eight hundred rooms.

Over many centuries great societies develop and then disappear, leaving bits of their art and science which we can see today. The Mayas and the Aztecs, in what is now

Mexico and Central America, develop art, architecture, a written language, astronomy and mathematics. They use the zero in mathematics hundreds of years before the Europeans learn how. They make a calendar which is in some ways more exact than the one we use today.

Perhaps most important: The People, in all their many cultures, believe that they are part of Nature. The earth is the mother of everything that lives and Mother Earth belongs to everyone.

For thousands of years The People are the only humans living in North and Central and South America. That time comes to an end. In boats with oars or ships with many sails, Europeans begin to cross the ocean. It is their turn to discover the New World.

Chapter One, Overview

The Explorers [1]

Until the time they sail away and discover [2] America, Europeans live in a small world. Most people live all their short lives without leaving the villages where they are born. They have very little education and almost no science. Fear of the unknown [3] keeps them close to home. Some people still believe the earth is flat, and that anyone foolish enough to go to the edge may fall off. Finally, geographers [4] understand that the earth is round, not flat, so it is not possible to fall off. But even sailors of long experience are afraid to sail on "The Green Sea of Darkness," as they call the Atlantic Ocean. They believe that sea monsters [5] and other awful dangers are waiting there.

Fortunately, there are always a few brave, curious people who have the courage to travel a little farther from the shores [6] of home. In the eighth, ninth and tenth centuries, the big, violent Scandinavian Vikings are the best ship builders and sailors in the world. One of them, Eric the Red, sails from Norway in about 950 and discovers Greenland. Fifty years later, Eric's son, Leif Ericson, sails out in one of those fast, brightly painted Viking ships and arrives at a land he calls Vinland, or Wineland,

Norsemen voyages

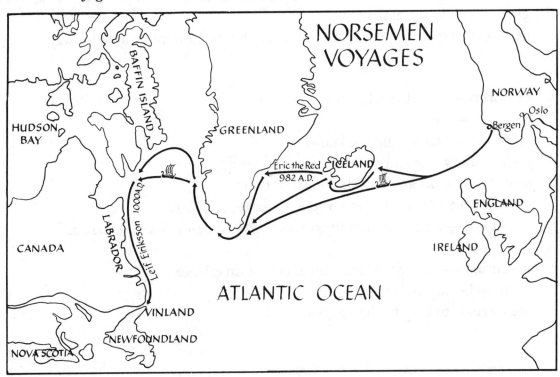

Library of Congress

Vikings sailing from Greenland

because there are wild grapes growing there. We now know that Vinland is in North America. Leif Ericson is probably the first European explorer ever to visit that continent[7].

Two hundred and fifty years after Leif Ericson visits Vinland, two Italian brothers, Nicolo and Maffeo Polo, travel east by land to China. They are the first Europeans to go to the continent of Asia. Their journey is long and dangerous, but they return home with wonderful stories to tell. Nicolo goes to China again, this time with his son, Marco. Marco Polo writes a book about his adventures[8] in China which, two hundred years later, another Italian explorer, Christopher Columbus, reads again and again.

Trade[9] begins between Europe and the Orient, or eastern part of the world. Rich Europeans now have a desire to buy the enjoyable things that come from the countries of the Orient, especially China and India: silks, perfume, beautiful rugs and spices. In this time before refrigeration, there is a great need for spices to preserve[10] food. But the greatest desire is to find gold.

Because it is so difficult to reach the Orient by land, explorers look for ways to get there by sea.

[1] **explorers** — travelers who go to unknown places
[2] **discover** — find
[3] **unknown** — something not known
[4] **geographers** — scientists who study the earth
[5] **monster** — a big and terrible animal or thing
[6] **shore** — the edge of the land where it touches the water
[7] **continent** — a large main land area, as North America, South America, Australia, etc.
[8] **adventure** — an exciting and /or dangerous experience
[9] **trade** — buying and selling
[10] **preserve** — to keep fresh and good

Chapter One, Overview
The Explorers

Exercises

A. **Reading Comprehension — Discussion and Writing.** Choose three of these questions to discuss with a partner. Write the rest of the answers. You may look back and copy them from the story, or write them in your own words.

1. Why are the sailors afraid to sail on the Atlantic Ocean?

_____

_____

_____

2. Who are the best ship builders during the eighth, ninth and tenth centuries?

_____

_____

_____

3. When they sail from Norway, what discovery do the Vikings make?

_____

_____

_____

4. When they travel over land, to what country do the Italian Polo brothers go?

_____

_____

_____

5. What things do rich Europeans want from the Orient?

_____

_____

_____

B.   Vocabulary. Fill in the blanks with the correct word.

1. Great _____ of the unknown keeps people close to home.

2. Marco Polo writes a book about his_____ in China.

3. There is a special need for _____ to preserve food.

4. _____ look for ways to get to the Orient by sea.

C.   Definitions. Draw a line between words on the left and right that have nearly the same meaning.

1. explorers   a. adventure

2. land at the edge of the water   b. discover

3. an exciting experience   c. buying and selling

4. trade   d. travelers who go to an unknown place

5. to find something   e. shore

Chapter One, Story

Christopher Columbus: The Grand Admiral of the Ocean Sea (Part One)

His name is Cristoforo Colombo in Italian, Cristobal or Cristoval Colon in Spanish, and Christopher Columbus in English. He is born in Genoa, Italy, in 1451, the son of poor parents. He studies astronomy[12], navigation[13], history and Latin. While he is still quite young his father sends him to sea to become a sailor.

Over and over again, young Columbus reads Marco Polo's famous book of travels in the Orient. Columbus is intelligent and ambitious[14]. He dreams of honor, wealth and power. A sure way to get them, he believes, is to discover a sea route, a way by sea, to the riches[15] of China and the East Indies. The East Indies is the name for India, Indochina and their nearby islands.

When he is twenty-eight years old, Columbus goes to live in Portugal. There he has the good fortune to marry a young woman whose family is rich and has many important friends. One of these friends introduces Columbus to King John II of Portugal.

For months and years, Columbus asks King John to give him money, to support him in a voyage[16] of exploration and discovery. Because he knows the world is round, Columbus believes that the best way to reach the Far East is to sail west. Columbus is sure that the eastern coast of China is only about three thousand miles away, across the Atlantic Ocean. Neither Columbus nor anyone else living at that time understands that all of North and South America and the great, wide Pacific Ocean lie between Portugal and China. The king finally agrees to help Columbus with his voyage and asks him what he wants if he succeeds.

Columbus knows exactly what he wants. He wants to be called Grand Admiral of the Ocean Sea. He wants authority[17] over any lands he discovers. He hopes to keep for himself one-tenth of any gold that he finds.

The king is angry. He thinks Columbus demands[18] too much. He refuses to support the voyage, and Columbus is no longer a welcome visitor.

Columbus is disappointed[19]. He leaves Portugal and goes to Spain. He again looks for important friends who can introduce him to the Spanish king, Ferdinand, and the queen, Isabella. He finally gets what he wants. After they say "no" for a long time, and after they say "maybe" for a long time, the king and queen of Spain agree to help Columbus. They are going to pay most of the expenses of his voyage to the Orient.

Christopher Columbus

11 **admiral** — the highest officer in the navy
12 **astronomy** — science of the stars
13 **navigation** — to direct the route of a ship
14 **ambitious** — having a strong desire for success
15 **riches** — land, or money, or valuable possessions
16 **voyage** — travel by water
17 **authority** — the right to command, or be master
18 **demand** — ask for, very strongly
19 **disappointed** — having hopes that are not satisfied

Chapter One, Story
Christopher Columbus (Part One)

Exercises

A. **Reading Comprehension — Writing and Discussion.** Choose three questions for discussion with a partner. Write the rest of the answers. You may look back and copy them from the story, or write them in your own words.

1. How does Columbus plan to get honor, wealth and power?

   _____

   _____

   _____

2. How does Columbus plan to reach the Far East? Why does he want to go that way?

   _____

   _____

   _____

3. How far away does Columbus believe the east coast of China is from Europe?

   _____

   _____

   _____

4. What things does Columbus want if he succeeds in discovering the route to the Orient?

   _____

   _____

   _____

5. Who is going to pay for Columbus' voyage?

_____

_____

_____

B.   Vocabulary. Fill in the blanks with the correct word.

1. His father sends him to sea to become a _____.

2. Columbus is intelligent and _____.

3. Columbus is sure that the eastern coast of China is only about_____ away.

4. He wants to be called _____.

5. He goes to Spain and again begins to look for _____ friends.

C.   Definitions. Write the word you can use instead of the underlined phrases.

1. Columbus dreams of honor, wealth and power. He is _____.

2. King John refuses to give Columbus money for the voyage. He refuses to _____ the voyage.

3. Columbus wants to be the master of the lands he discovers. He wants _____ over lands he discovers.

Chapter One, Story

Christopher Columbus: The Grand Admiral of the Ocean Sea (Part Two)

On August 3, 1492, with three small ships and ninety men, Christopher Columbus sails out of the little port[20] of Palos, Spain. As the Spanish coast gets smaller and smaller behind him, Columbus is beginning a brave voyage across a completely unknown and unfriendly ocean.

For a while, all goes well on the Nina, the Pinta and the Santa Maria, as the ships are called. But as day follows day with no land in sight, old fears of monsters and boiling seas return to frighten the sailors. They want to turn around and go home. On October 10, Columbus promises to sail back to Spain if he doesn't find land in two or three days.

On the morning of October 12, a sailor on the Pinta is looking out over the water and suddenly sees land! Columbus is now near one of the islands[21] close to Cuba and Haiti, but he thinks he is near the coast of Japan. It is a moment of sweet victory for him.

Wearing their finest clothes, and carrying the flags of the king and queen of Spain, the Spaniards march up the shore of the island (one of the Bahamas that we now call Watling Island) and name it San Salvador. The people who meet them are not wearing silk, and their homes are very different from what the Spaniards expect, but Columbus is still sure that the next, bigger island (Cuba) is Japan.

Now everything begins to go wrong. The king and queen expect Columbus to return to Spain with trunks full of gold, but he can't find

Spanish galleons

UCLA

9

much gold, so he takes slaves[22], instead.

When Columbus sails back to Spain, after his first voyage, he gets a hero's welcome. He is given the power to govern these new Spanish possessions. But after a second and a third voyage he becomes less popular[23]. Where is the gold of the Orient that Columbus is supposed to bring back? Are these voyages worth[24] all the trouble and expense? Queen Isabella hears that native people on the islands are being treated very cruelly[25]. During his third voyage, she sends someone to arrest Columbus and bring him back to Spain in chains.

The queen forgives[26] him, but Columbus is now a sad man, tired, sick, and almost forgotten by everyone. He dies in 1506, still thinking that he is the discoverer of the sea route to Japan, still not understanding that he is the discoverer of a New World.

[20] **port** — a harbor; a city where ships can enter

[21] **island** — a small land area, with water all around

[22] **slave** — a person who is owned by and works for another person without pay

[23] **popular** — liked by many people

[24] **worth** — (the trouble and expense) — valuable enough (for the trouble and expense)

[25] **cruelly** — badly, unkindly

[26] **forgive** — pardon, excuse

The Voyages of Columbus

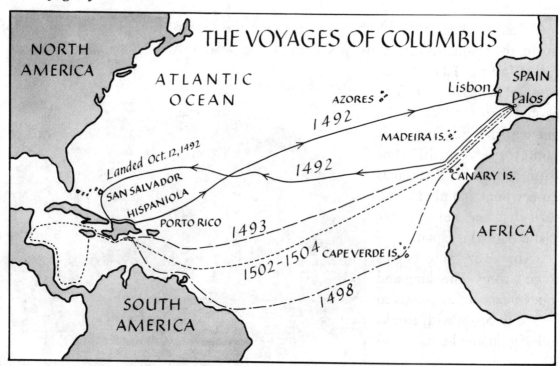

Chapter One, Story
Christopher Columbus (Part Two)

Exercises

A. **Reading Comprehension — Discussion and Writing.** Choose two questions for discussion with a partner. Write the rest, looking back at the story or using your own words.

1. What are the names of Columbus' ships?

_____

_____

_____

2. Where are Columbus' ships when they finally see land?

_____

_____

_____

3. What does Columbus want to bring to the king and queen of Spain? What does he really bring to them?

_____

_____

_____

4. Why does Columbus become less popular as time goes by?

_____

_____

_____

B. **Vocabulary.** Fill in the blanks with the correct word.

1. Old fears of monsters and boiling seas return to _____ the sailors.

2. Columbus believes that he is close to one of the islands off the _____ of Japan.

3. After his first voyage he gets a _____ welcome.

4. They bring him back to Spain in _____.

5. He is the _____ of the New World.

C. Definitions. Fill in the blanks with words you remember from your reading.

1. The sailors think about monsters and boiling seas. They have_____ that make them want to turn around and go home.

2. Columbus does not bring gold back to Spain, and he is a very bad governor. He becomes less _____ as time goes by.

Chapter Two, Overview

Coming to America

Fifty years after the death of Columbus, Spain becomes the master of the New World. In Mexico and Peru, the Spanish at last find the gold and silver of Columbus' dreams. The treasures they take make Spain the most powerful nation on earth.

England at this time is just a small country of farms and villages. Its most important city, London, has a population[1] of only 75,000 people. The English are not yet strong enough to take a piece of America for themselves. Still, they do try, toward the end of the sixteenth century. By then, the English have to take what the Spanish don't want: the land of rock and hill and forest north of Florida. This land later becomes the thirteen English colonies in North America.

The English king, Henry VIII, breaks away from the Roman Catholic church and establishes[2] the Protestant religion in England. Under Henry's daughter, Queen Elizabeth, England becomes a world power with a great navy. Not long after Elizabeth dies, the English finally establish their first North American settlement[3], Jamestown,

The first landing of the Pilgrims, 1620

Library of Congress

on the shores of Virginia. The year is 1607. Thirteen years later, a ship, the Mayflower, arrives in Massachusetts from England carrying one hundred and two men, women and children. These people call themselves Pilgrims[4] and they name their settlement Plymouth.

In the next twenty years, eighty thousand people cross over from the Old World to the New. The distance is great and the voyage is difficult. Life in the settlements is very hard. There is always danger from unfriendly Indians. Why do so many people leave their homes and villages and travel to a far-away place they know nothing about?

Many of them come against their will[5]. The first ship carrying black people arrives in Jamestown in 1619, even before the Pilgrims. These blacks are called servants, but they are treated like slaves. Some white people come against their will, too: criminals[6], and people who owe money and must choose between going to America or going to prison. Most of those who come willingly want land, which they cannot own in Europe because much of the land already belongs to others. And there are some, like the Pilgrims, who come because they do not have freedom of religion in the Old World and hope to find it in America.

[1] **population** — all the people in a country
[2] **establish** — set up, or start something
[3] **settlement** — a small village
[4] **Pilgrim** — a person who travels a long distance, usually for a religious reason
[5] **against their will** — against their wish or desire
[6] **criminals** — people who act or do something against the law

Chapter Two, Overview
Coming to America

Exercises

A. **Reading Comprehension — Discussion and Writing.** Choose two of these questions to discuss with a partner. Write the rest of the answers. You may look back and copy them from the story, or write them in your own words.

1. About 50 years after Columbus' death, how does Spain become a powerful nation?

_____

_____

_____

2. Where do the English establish their first settlements?

_____

_____

_____

3. Give reasons why so many people come to the settlements.

_____

_____

_____

★ ★ ★ ★ ★ ★ ★ ★ ★ ★ ★ ★ ★ ★ ★ ★ ★ ★ ★

B. **Vocabulary.** Fill in the correct word using the list below:

master   religion   freedom

treasure   establishes   settlements

1. King Henry VIII breaks from the Roman Catholic _____ and _____ a Protestant one in England.

2. The _____ of silver and gold that Spain takes makes it _____ of the New World.

3. Life is not easy in the new _____, but many hope to find _____ of religion there.

C. **Definitions.** Choose an answer similar in meaning to the underlined word or words.

1. England's most important city, London, has very few <u>people</u> at this time. It has a small _____.

2. Under Queen Elizabeth, England becomes <u>strong and important in the world</u>. It becomes a _____.

3. The <u>men, women and children travel great distances</u> to find religious freedom. They are _____.

4. Many who come to the New World at this time are servants or slaves, and <u>do not wish</u> to be there. They are there _____.

5. Those who want a new life come there <u>gladly and freely</u>. They come there _____.

Chapter Two, Story One

The First Thanksgiving

At the beginning of the sixteenth century, the religion of all of Europe is Roman Catholic. By the end of the sixteenth century, many European countries, including England, are Protestant. Some English Protestants call themselves Puritans, from the word pure, because they want to keep Protestant churches pure of Roman Catholic influence[7].

It is easy to know, just by looking, who is a Puritan and who is not. At this time, most Englishmen have long hair and wear bright-colored clothes. But Puritan men cut their hair short and wear dark colors. Puritan women cover their heads with white caps and dress very plainly.

As the years pass, some Puritans become unhappy with the other Protestant churches. They especially do not trust the official[8] Church of England, of which the king, himself, is the head. It can be very dangerous not to belong to the king's own church. One group of Puritans, hoping to find greater religious freedom, decides to leave England and to go to Virginia. They believe that in the New World, far from the Church of England and the English king, they can safely practice their own religion in their own way. They call themselves Pilgrims because they are going on a very long voyage.

In the autumn of the year 1620, one hundred and two Pilgrims crowd into a small ship, the Mayflower, and sail away from England, from home, from everything and everyone they love.

On December 21, after sixty-six rough days at sea, the Mayflower lands off the coast of what is later to be

The First Thanksgiving

Library of Congress

the colony[9] of Massachusetts. They name the place where they land Plymouth, to remind them of Plymouth, England. It is now too late in the year, and too cold, to follow the original plan and continue down the coast to Virginia. Here they are in Plymouth, and here they decide to stay.

The first winter in Plymouth is a time of terrible hunger, suffering and death. Forty-eight of the one hundred and two Pilgrims die. Those who are strong enough bury the dead secretly, at night, to keep the Indians from learning how few of them are left. Everyone lives in fear of an attack by the Indians. But it doesn't happen. Instead, an Indian steps out of the forest one day and says, "Welcome."

This is Samoset, whose few English words come from meeting English fishermen farther up the coast. Samoset introduces the Pilgrim leaders to Massasoit, the chief of the local[10] Indian tribe[11]. Massasoit becomes a good and true friend to the Pilgrims. He sends another Indian, Squanto, who speaks English well, to help them. Squanto teaches the Pilgrims to grow corn the Indian way, by putting a fish in the earth with the corn seed to feed the young plant. He also shows them how to catch lobster and other sea food — which the English never learn to like, but eat to keep from being hungry.

In the spring, the Mayflower returns to England, and the Pilgrims are left to care for themselves. Slowly, conditions begin to get better. By the autumn of 1621, eleven houses are ready to live in and the corn is growing high. The first year is over and the Plymouth settlement, though small in numbers, is bravely looking toward the future.

It is time for the Pilgrims to give thanks to God. The first Thanksgiving takes place in late October or early November. Massasoit comes with ninety Indians and a gift of five deer. The Pilgrims play old English games and the Indians dance. They all eat together and enjoy white bread and probably roast wild turkey.

The peace between the Pilgrims and the Indians lasts only fifty years. Then Massasoit's son, King Phillip, begins to understand that the English intend to take the Indians' land. The settlers think that Indians are less than human, that they don't know how to use the good land they have, and shouldn't have it. King Phillip joins with other Indian tribes to make bloody war against the whites. He fights long and hard, but in the end, the colonists find him and kill him.

---

[7] **influence** — the effect something has on something else

[8] **official** — authorized: by authority (of the king)

[9] **colony** — a settlement of people in a new place, under the rule of another country

[10] **local** — of a certain, particular small place

[11] **tribe** — a group of people who come from the same forefathers

Chapter Two, Story One
The First Thanksgiving

Exercises

A. Reading Comprehension. Read the following sentences. Circle true or false. Write the sentences from the story that explain your answer.

1. True or False?

   The Puritans are not happy in England because they do not have religious freedom.

   _____

   _____

2. True or False?

   The Mayflower finally lands in Virginia.

   _____

   _____

3. True or False?

   During the first winter in Plymouth, the Indians attack the Pilgrims, and many Pilgrims die.

   _____

   _____

4. True or False?

   They live in peace together, because the Indians know the whites intend to take their land.

   _____

   _____

B.   Vocabulary. Fill in the correct word using the list below:

colony	Puritans	voyage	Catholic	religious	few
secretly	attacking	Thanksgiving		influence	dead	Roman

1. Some English Protestants are _____ and want to keep their churches pure of _____ _____ _____.

2. Pilgrims hope to find _____ freedom in the New World.

3. Plymouth is later to be in the _____ of Massachusetts.

4. They land after a long _____ of 66 rough days at sea.

5. The Pilgrims bury their _____ at night _____ so the Indians won't know how _____ of them are left.

6. The first _____ takes place in late October or early November.

C.   Fill in the blanks with words you remember from your reading.

The [1.]_____, who are unhappy with the Protestant Church of England, hope to find religious [2.]_____ in the [3.]_____. They call themselves [4.]_____ because they are going on a long [5.]_____. The first winter is a terrible time of hunger, suffering and [6.]_____. At first they fear an [7.]_____ by Indians. But the Indians become good friends to the Pilgrims and [8.]_____ them how to live in the forest.

After the [9.]_____ leaves for England, the Pilgrims have to care for [10.]_____.

To the first Thanksgiving, the Indians bring a gift of five [11.]_____. They all play [12.]_____ and dance and eat. Years later, the Indians understand that the whites [13.]_____ to take their lands.

20

Roger Williams and the Founding[12] of Rhode Island

The Puritans who come to the New World to find freedom of religion want it for themselves. They don't want to give it to anybody else. Catholics, Jews, even Protestants who think a little differently, are not welcome in the New England settlements.

Roger Williams, a young Puritan minister, sails from England to Boston, Massachusetts, in 1631. He has very independent[13] ideas and strongly questions the right of any government to establish a religion, or to control religious thinking. He believes that church and state must be separate. He believes that the only purpose of government is to keep the peace and to take care of the best interests of the people.

Williams' ideas anger Boston authorities, churchmen and judges. They force him to leave Massachusetts.

The Indian Chief Massasoit takes Williams in. The two men become friends. Williams lives with other Indians, too. He travels among them, learns to speak with them, and uses his influence to try to keep peaceful relations with them. Years later, he writes a study of Indian languages. He understands Indian problems. Williams believes that the king has no legal[14] right to give to the settlers land that belongs to the Indians. When he expresses this belief, which he does freely, he becomes unpopular with settlers who own land.

Roger Williams

In 1636, Roger Williams builds the settlement of Providence on land that he buys from the Indians. This is the beginning of a new colony: Rhode Island. To Rhode Island come those people who are not content[15] in other settlements because of religious or political differences. All are welcome.

In its first days, Rhode Island is an example of popular government[16] unknown in this period anywhere in the world. The form of government is simple: a town meeting of heads of families gets together every two weeks to discuss "the common peace and planting." The constitution of Rhode Island contains the words, "All men may walk as their consciences[17] persuade them, every one in the name of God." For this period [18] in history, these are unbelievably modern words.

★ ★ ★ ★ ★ ★ ★ ★ ★ ★ ★ ★ ★ ★ ★ ★ ★ ★ ★ ★

Because of Roger Williams, Rhode Island is close to being a democracy. It is as close as colonial America is going to be for a long, long time.

[12] **found** — to begin to build
[13] **independent** — not influenced by other people
[14] **legal** — permitted by law
[15] **content (or contented)** — satisfied
[16] **popular government** — democracy — government by the people generally
[17] **conscience(s)** — knowledge or sense of what is right and wrong
[18] **period** — a definite time

Chapter Two, Story Two
Roger Williams and the Founding of Rhode Island

Exercises

A. **Reading Comprehension — Discussion and Writing.** Choose two of these questions to discuss with a partner. Write the rest of the answers. You may look back and copy them from the story, or write them in your own words.

1. What does Roger Williams believe to be the purpose of government?

    _____

    _____

    _____

2. Why do the Boston authorities force Roger Williams to leave Massachusetts?

    _____

    _____

    _____

3. Who does Roger Williams believe owns the land?

    _____

    _____

    _____

4. Which people are welcome in the new colony of Rhode Island?

    _____

    _____

    _____

5. What kind of government does Rhode Island have?

_____

_____

_____

B.   Vocabulary. Find a word from the story to complete these sentences.

1. The ᵃ·_____ want freedom of religion for themselves, but they do not give it to others.

2. Roger Williams believes that ᵇ·_____ and ᶜ·_____ must be separate.

3. Roger Williams believes that the king of England cannot give away land to settlers in the New World because it ᵈ·_____ to the ᵉ·_____.

4. Democracy is ᶠ·_____ government.

Chapter Three, Overview

Storm Clouds over the Colonies

In 1760, George III becomes the new king of Great Britain[1], of which England is a part. The American colonies, three thousand miles away, belong to Great Britain. Because of this great distance, American colonists govern themselves much of the time. More and more they like the idea of self-government.

When the British need money to pay for a long and expensive war with France, they try to get it by taxing the colonies. Many colonists argue that these taxes[2] are not fair. Nobody from America is a member of the British government, so nobody from America ever gets to vote for or against such taxes. A popular saying is, "No taxation without representation[3]."

Foolishly, the king sends soldiers to force the colonies to obey the tax laws. Even the colonists who are still faithful[4] to the king and his government hate to see British soldiers marching down their streets. The people call the soldiers "redcoats" and "lobster-backs" because they wear bright red uniform jackets over their white pants. Naturally, the soldiers don't like people who call them names. Bad feelings grow on both sides.

[1] **Great Britain** — England, Scotland and Wales together
[2] **taxes** — money that people pay to support their government
[3] **representation** — having someone to speak or act for a group
[4] **faithful** — true to or loyal

Chapter Three, Overview
Storm Clouds over the Colonies

Exercises

A. **Reading Comprehension — Discussion and Writing.** Choose one question to discuss with a partner. Write answers to the other questions, using your own words or copying them from the story.

1. Why do Great Britain's American colonies want to govern themselves?

    _____

    _____

    _____

2. Why don't the colonies vote against British taxes?

    _____

    _____

    _____

3. How does King George force the colonists to pay taxes?

    _____

    _____

    _____

B. **Vocabulary. Fill in the blanks with the correct word.**

1. England is part of _____.

2. American colonists _____ themselves because they are far from Britain.

3. No colonists can vote for or against British taxes because they are not _____ of the British government.

4. The king sends his soldiers to the colonies to force them to _____ the tax laws.

C. **Definitions.** Choose an answer for the <u>underlined words</u> that make the meaning clear.

1. American colonists, far away from Great Britain, like the idea of <u>ruling themselves</u>. They like _____.

2. The British government wants money from the colonists to <u>pay for its war expenses</u>. It wants them to pay _____.

3. American colonists don't think it is right to have to pay taxes that <u>they can't vote for or against</u>. They don't have_____.

Chapter Three, Story One

The Boston Massacre[5]

On March 5, 1770, a heavy snow falls over Boston, Massachusetts. It's a school holiday so there are many boys in the street making snowballs. Some of the boys throw snowballs at the British soldiers. One soldier hits a boy with the flat side of his sword[6]. A crowd gathers and soon hundreds of angry colonists are yelling insults at the soldiers. A few throw stones. "Lobster, lobster, you dare[7] not fire!" they shout.

UCLA

The Boston Massacre by Paul Revere

But the British soldiers do fire their guns. Five colonists lie dead or dying, among them Crispus Attucks, a run-away black slave. History remembers this as the Boston Massacre.

After the Boston Massacre, some citizens talk openly about a very new and dangerous idea: liberty. The idea of independence from England spreads. There are "Liberty trees" in many towns and villages. People wear "Liberty caps" and, in Boston, a lawyer named Samuel Adams starts an organization he calls "Sons of Liberty." The men who belong to this organization do their best to make life unpleasant for redcoats, for British officials, and for American colonists who are still faithful to the king.

Sam Adams has little money, and never succeeds either as a lawyer or in any business that he tries. But he is very successful as a political[8] leader. He and his cousin, John Adams, a future president of the United States, support American independence. Both Samuel and John Adams represent Massachusetts in an important meeting in Philadelphia in 1774. The meeting is the First Continental Congress. There, for the first time, representatives from all the colonies meet to demand justice from King George.

Sam Adams sits at the back of the big meeting room. He listens carefully to all the speeches. Some of the speakers, including calm, sensible George Washington of Virginia, still hope for an agreement with the king's government. Adams just sits, listens, and says little. In his heart he knows that the colonies are not going to get justice from the king. Independence is what they need, and that means war — the little American colonies against the most powerful country in the world.

Sam Adams

5 **massacre** — killing a large number of people, without pity

6 **sword** — a long knife, or blade, used in fighting

7 **dare (not)** — don't have the courage; aren't brave enough

8 **political** — of the government

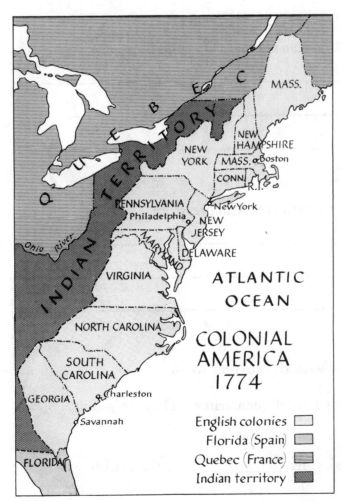

The thirteen original colonies, 1774

Chapter Three, Story One
The Boston Massacre

Exercises

A. **Reading Comprehension — Discussion and Writing.** Choose one question to discuss with a partner. Write answers to the other questions, using your own words or copying them from the story.

1. Why do the British soldiers fire their guns at the colonists?

   _____

   _____

   _____

2. What new idea comes to the American colonists after the Boston Massacre?

   _____

   _____

   _____

3. What is the reason for the First Continental Congress?

   _____

   _____

   _____

B. **Vocabulary. Fill in the blanks with the correct word.**

1. The colonists yell at the soldiers and call them names. They are yelling

   _____.

2. Sons of Liberty organize to make life _____ for the British.

3. Sam and John Adams go to the meeting of the First Continental Congress for Massachusetts. They_____ Massachusetts.

4. Some of the speakers there still hope to get an agreement from the king. They ask for_____.

C. **Definitions.** Draw a line between words on the left and right that have nearly the same meaning.

1. calls them names   a. faithful

2. liberty   b. insults

3. loyal   c. independence

4. redcoats   d. British soldiers

Chapter Three, Story Two

The Boston Tea Party

The British need money from the colonies to pay for wars, mostly against the French in Europe and in America. For this, they collect taxes. Each new tax causes more anger in the colonies until finally, in 1776, the British stop trying to collect taxes at all. But one way or the other, King George intends to teach the American colonists a lesson. Too many of them are trouble makers. Too few of them respect their king. They complain about every little thing. It is time for them to learn that they must obey British law whether they like it or not.

The colonists usually buy their tea wherever it is least expensive. But a new law, the Tea Act of 1773, makes it illegal to buy tea except from official British tea sellers. Since tea is the most popular drink in the colonies, there are thousands of tea drinkers who see that the new law is really a tax and is not fair. This is exactly the kind of situation Sam Adams and his friends like, because it makes ordinary American colonists enemies of the king. Adams writes letters to political leaders in the other colonies. He advises them not to allow British tea to come in. Paul Revere, one of the Sons of Liberty, delivers these letters for Adams, riding his horse night and day. Revere brings messages back from the other leaders. They are not going to allow British tea into their colonies, either.

On November 28, 1773, a ship from England carrying one hundred and nineteen boxes of tea arrives in Boston. A few weeks later, two other ships arrive with more tea. Signs go up on walls of Boston buildings announcing a town meeting to discuss what to do about the tea. Citizens crowd into the meeting hall. People are angry and they are getting angrier. Still the government refuses to listen.

On a cold, rainy night in December, a group of fifty young men, some of them Sons of Liberty, meet quietly and secretly in a house in Boston. There they dress in Indian clothes, put dark color on their faces

The Boston Tea Party, 1773

"Indian" throwing tea into the bay

and feathers in their hair. Then they march down to the harbor, climb into the three English ships, and throw three hundred and forty-two boxes of tea into the water. After that, singing songs, whistling, and feeling very proud[9] of themselves, they march back to town. The Boston Tea Party is over.

Of course, the feathers and the Indian clothes do not fool the British. They know perfectly well who is responsible for the Boston Tea Party. The king acts quickly to punish Boston. Until the town pays for the tea, the government refuses to allow any ship at all into Boston Harbor. This means that no food, no medicine, no necessary thing of any kind can enter the city. The king also sends four thousand soldiers to Boston, where people must let these hated redcoats sleep in their homes.

The British government believes that hunger, need, and fear of the soldiers will finally make the people of Boston obey the law. The British government is wrong. Paul Revere and other messengers like him race their horses to all the colonies. They spread the news of what is happening in Boston. Soon there is another Tea Party, this time in New York. And from New York, Connecticut, Virginia and South Carolina come gifts of rice, fish and money to keep the citizens of Boston alive. King George doesn't understand that, without meaning to, he is uniting the thirteen separate colonies into one single American nation[10].

[9] **proud** — with a good opinion
[10] **nation** — the people of one government

Chapter Three, Story Two
Boston Tea Party

Exercises

A. **Reading Comprehension — Discussion and Writing.** Choose two questions to discuss with a partner. Write answers to the other questions using your own words or copying them from the story.

1. Why do the British need money from the colonists?

_____

_____

_____

2. What do the colonists think about the Tea Act of 1773?

_____

_____

_____

3. What do the Sons of Liberty do secretly one night in December?

_____

_____

_____

4. How does King George try to punish the town of Boston?

_____

_____

_____

5. What is the result of King George's punishment?

_____

_____

_____

B. **Vocabulary.** Fill in the correct words using the list below.

Indian	Boston	uniting	leaders	collect
feathers	Party	obey	political	taxes	Tea

1. The king wants the colonies to help pay for Britain's wars against the French. That is why the British _____ _____.

2. Sam Adams writes important letters that Paul Revere delivers to the _____ _____ of the American colonies.

3. Fifty young men dress themselves as _____, with _____ in their hair, climb into the English ships, and throw boxes into the water. This is the _____ _____ _____

4. The king is very angry. He wants the colonists to _____ British law, so he sends many soldiers to Boston. He is _____ the colonists against Britain.

C. **Definitions.** Choose words from the story to complete the sentences.

1. King George wants to teach the colonists a lesson. He _____ to punish them for not obeying British law.

2. Everyone likes tea. It is a very _____ drink.

3. The king doesn't let any ships land in Boston until the colonists pay for the tea. He _____ _____ _____ ships to enter with any necessary things.

Chapter Three, Story Three

The Midnight Ride Of Paul Revere

In the spring of 1775, groups of men march and train[11] for war in almost every village. They call themselves "minutemen" because they say they can be ready in a minute to defend their towns and villages against the British.

General Gage, the commander of the king's army in Massachusetts, has information that the Americans are hiding guns and gunpowder[12] in the town of Concord, north of Boston. He also has information that Samuel Adams and his rich friend, John Hancock, are visiting in Lexington, a town between Boston and Concord. If he can catch them, King George intends to hang[13] Adams and Hancock for trying to start a revolution[14]. General Gage hopes to please the king by arresting Adams and Hancock and finding the guns and gunpowder, all at the same time.

Paul Revere by John Singleton Copley

Paul Revere learns what General Gage is planning to do. Revere needs to know how the general's seven hundred soldiers are going to get from Boston to Concord. If they leave Boston by boat, they are going to use one road. If they leave Boston by land, they are going to use a different road. It is important for Paul Revere to know which way the redcoats are coming. He must tell the minutemen where to stop them before they get to Concord.

Revere arranges for[15] a friend to send a signal from the top of a tall Boston church. The friend is going to show one light if the British are coming by land, two lights if they are coming by water.

Meanwhile, Revere crosses the river in a small boat and waits in the dark on the other side. Time passes. No light shows at the top of the tall church. More time passes. Still no light. Then Revere sees the signal. One light — no, two lights! The redcoats are coming across the river!

He quickly tells the other American messengers who ride off into the night to warn the towns and villages near Concord. Revere himself races to Lexington to wake up Adams and Hancock and help them get away safely. Then, as fast as his horse will travel, Revere continues on toward Concord, stopping only to tell the villages he passes that the redcoats are coming.

Paul Revere's Ride, painting by Grant Wood

Paul Revere doesn't get as far as Concord. British soldiers catch him on the road and take him prisoner. But they let him go because they suddenly find themselves in the middle of completely unexpected gunfire. In the darkness of night, farmers and minutemen arrive from everywhere. They shoot at the redcoats from behind trees, bushes, houses, wagons. The British are not used to this kind of fighting.

This is the famous battle of Lexington and Concord. It is the first battle of the American Revolution and, to their own surprise, the Americans win it.

[11] **train** — to practice
[12] **gunpowder** — a powder that explodes, blows up, used to shoot guns
[13] **hang** — to kill someone, putting a rope around someone's neck and suspending him until dead
[14] **revolution** — a fight by the people to overthrow their government
[15] **arranges** (for) — prepares (for)

Chapter Three, Story Three
The Midnight Ride of Paul Revere

Exercises

A. **Reading Comprehension — Discussion and Writing.** Choose two questions to discuss with a partner. Write answers to the other questions using your own words or copying from the story.

1. Who are the minutemen and what do they intend to do?

   _____

   _____

   _____

2. What does General Gage think is going to please the king?

   _____

   _____

   _____

3. What is the signal to tell Paul Revere how the redcoats are coming to Concord?

   _____

   _____

   _____

4. What important thing happens that stops Paul Revere from getting to Concord?

   _____

   _____

   _____

B. **Vocabulary.** Fill in the correct words from the story.

1. Minutemen can be ready in a minute to _____ their country.

2. Paul Revere needs to know if the redcoats are coming by land or water. He _____ for a friend to send a signal of light.

3. The minutemen must ride off into the night _____ the towns and villages that the redcoats are coming.

4. The British soldiers are surprised by completely _____ gunfire.

C. **Definitions.** Draw a line to match the words on the left with the words on the right.

1. group   a. taking a person, under the law, as a prisoner

2. hanging   b. a number of people together

3. arresting   c. a sign

4. signal   d. a way of killing someone

5. planning   e. thinking out an idea

Birth of a Nation

After the surprising victory at Lexington and Concord, more and more colonists support the idea of independence from England. However, most of them still hope to settle their quarrel[1] with King George without separating from England. Between the spring of 1775 and the summer of 1776 two things happen to change public opinion.

In May, 1775, British warships threaten[2] the city of Boston. To protect it, Americans occupy Bunker Hill, near Boston. The Americans are few, with few guns. The British are many, with many guns. The king's soldiers, in their beautiful red and white uniforms, march up the hill in perfectly straight rows. Some of the Americans don't even have uniforms. They are just farm boys who spend a week or two training for war, fighting, and who then go home again to plant corn. But their officers are experienced and know exactly what to do with the little gunpowder they have. They wait and wait until the first row of redcoats comes marching up the hill and is getting quite close to them.

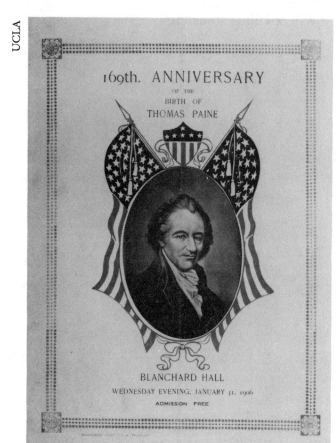

169th. ANNIVERSARY

OF THE

BIRTH OF

THOMAS PAINE

BLANCHARD HALL

WEDNESDAY EVENING, JANUARY 31, 1906

ADMISSION FREE

"Don't fire until you see the whites of their eyes," one officer commands.

The British win the Battle of Bunker Hill, but only after the Americans have nothing left to shoot. In the end, almost half the British soldiers are dead or wounded, hurt very badly. After this battle, Americans realize for the first time that they really have a chance to beat the British.

The second event that changes public opinion happens in the winter of 1776. Thomas Paine, a recent immigrant[3] to America from England, writes a little book he calls "Common Sense." Tom Paine is a clear thinker who supports the American

Thomas Paine

★ ★ ★ ★ ★ ★ ★ ★ ★ ★ ★ ★ ★ ★ ★ ★ ★ ★ ★ ★

Revolution with all his heart. "Common Sense" makes a powerful argument for liberty, justice and independence. Hundreds of thousands of copies are sold in the first year. People who know how to read, and even those who don't, buy the book and talk about it with growing excitement.

Meanwhile, in Philadelphia, the Continental Congress is meeting. The fifty-six men who are there represent each of the thirteen colonies. Some of them are ready to vote for independence, some are not.

1   **quarrel** — disagreement, in an angry way; an argument
2   **threaten** — intend to hurt
3   **immigrant** — a person who comes to live in a new country

Chapter Four, Overview
Birth of a Nation

Exercises

A. **Reading Comprehension — Discussion and Writing.** Choose two questions to discuss with a partner. Write the answers to the rest, using your own words or copying them from the story.

1. When is the first time the colonists realize they can win a war with Britain?

_____

_____

_____

2. What is "Common Sense" and how does it influence public opinion?

_____

_____

_____

3. Why does an American officer command, "Don't shoot till you see the whites of their eyes"?

_____

_____

_____

4. What are the 56 representatives going to talk about at the Continental Congress?

_____

_____

_____

B. **Vocabulary.** Fill in the blanks with words from the story.

1. Even after the victory at Lexington and Concord, many American colonists want to settle their quarrel without _____ from England.

2. American farm boys do not have much experience in war. They spend a little time _____ for war. They don't wear _____, and they have very little _____ to shoot.

3. Thomas Paine comes to America from England. He is an _____.

C. **Definitions.** What do the following words mean? Look them up in your dictionary, and then write each one in a sentence. Discuss your answers.

1. separate

_____

_____

2. wound

_____

_____

3. realize

_____

_____

4. independence

_____

_____

Chapter Four, Story One

The Declaration of Independence

The Second Continental Congress meets in Philadelphia on May 10, 1776. Sam Adams and John Hancock travel there secretly from Massachusetts. They know the British still intend to hang them. Benjamin Franklin, the famous statesman and scientist, represents Pennsylvania. George Washington and Thomas Jefferson, wealthy landowners whom everyone respects, represent Virginia.

For weeks and months the congress talks and argues and tries to decide: is it best for the American colonies to become independent of England or is it not? The first time congress votes on this question, the vote is seven colonies for independence, six against. After the Battle of Bunker Hill, and after "Common Sense," the vote is ten for independence and three against. Then, in the spring of 1776, there is news that shocks everyone. The British are planning to attack New York. This threat helps to change those three votes. All thirteen colonies agree. The time for independence is now!

Thomas Jefferson, thirty-three years old, has the job of preparing a Declaration of Independence. Working alone in a rented room, he writes one of the most important documents, or official papers, of modern times.

The Declaration of Independence says, declares, that all men are created[5] equal.

It says that all men are born with certain natural rights. They have the right to life, liberty, and the pursuit[6] of happiness.

It says that the purpose of government is to protect these rights. If government fails to do this, the people have the right to change it.

On July 2, Thomas Jefferson presents his Declaration of Independence to the congress. The other representatives change some of Jefferson's words, and they take out completely a part in which he discusses the slave trade. Though he himself owns slaves, Jefferson is not comfortable with the idea of slavery. He wants the new United States of America to stop the buying and selling of black Africans. There are others in congress who agree with Jefferson, but not enough of them.

The final Declaration, a work of many compromises[7], is accepted by the whole congress on July 4, 1776. On July 8 there is a great celebration. Church bells ring out all over the land. This is the day that the United States of America declares to the world that it is free and independent.

The Declaration of Independence is carefully copied and on August 2 it is ready for the representatives in congress to sign. John Hancock shows his defiance[8] of King George by writing his name larger than any of the others — to make it easy, he jokes, for the king to find him without putting on his glasses. Actually, it is no joke. Every man who signs the Declaration is now in as much danger from the British as Sam Adams and John Hancock.

"There must be no pulling different ways," John Hancock warns. "We must all hang together."*

Wise old Ben Franklin replies, "Yes, we must all hang together or we shall all hang separately."

* "We must all stay together."

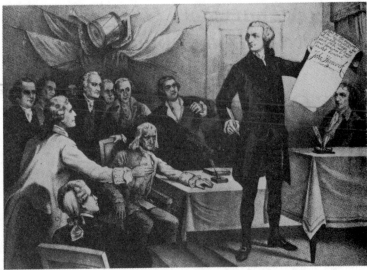

John Hancock's defiance

5 **create** — bring into (life) being
6 **pursuit** — the search for
7 **compromise** — agreement of two sides, in an argument; to go half way, in an argument
8 **defiance** — opposition to something

The Declaration of Independence at Philadelphia, July 4, 1776
Thomas Jefferson holding paper, center; left to right: John Adams, Roger Sherman, Robert Livingston, Benjamin Franklin

Chapter Four, Story One
The Declaration of Independence

Exercises

A. **Reading Comprehension — Discussion and Writing.** Choose one question to discuss with a partner. Write the answers to the others, using your own words or copying them from the story.

1. What three important things happen to make all thirteen colonies want to become independent from England?

_____

_____

_____

2. What natural rights does the Declaration of Independence say all people have?

_____

_____

_____

3. Why is the Declaration of Independence a work of compromise?

_____

_____

_____

B.   Vocabulary. Draw a line to relate the words on the left with the words on the right.

1. liberty   a. states

2. representatives   b. document

3. Declaration of Independence   c. statesmen

4. colonies   d. congress

5. government   e. freedom

C.   Definitions. Choose one word that has a similar meaning to <u>underlined</u> words.

1. Sam Adams and John Hancock know they are in danger because the British <u>plan to</u> hang them if they catch them. The British _____ to kill them.

2. If the new government <u>can not and does not</u> protect people, they have a right to change that government. Citizens can change the government when it _____ to protect them.

3. All of the representatives finally <u>agree, and settle their arguments</u>. They _____ to accept the Declaration of Independence.

Chapter Four, Story Two

Washington at Valley Forge

One of the few things that all the members of congress agree about is that George Washington of Virginia is the right man to lead the American army. Washington is calm, quiet and has a good reputation[9] as an officer. Also, he is rich enough that he can afford to serve without pay. This is important because the congress has almost no money.

In 1777, Washington wins some big victories, but he is not able to keep the British from taking Philadelphia. This is a very serious loss to the Americans. The members of congress, now meeting in Philadelphia, must get out of the city as fast as they can. Washington and his army of fifteen thousand men go to Valley Forge, twenty miles from Philadelphia, where Washington decides to stay for the winter. One of the reasons for choosing Valley Forge is that many trees grow there. The soldiers can cut them down to use for firewood and also to build small houses for themselves.

The British stay in Philadelphia that winter. They are happy and comfortable there. They have good food to eat, warm beds to sleep in, pretty women to dance with at holiday parties.

While the British are resting and enjoying themselves, American soldiers at Valley Forge suffer terrible cold and hunger. The money that the new United States government prints is not worth much. Farmers don't want to accept it as payment for meat and corn. Some farmers are secretly selling food to the British army whose money is worth more. For many weeks, Washington's men have nothing to eat but "fire cakes" which they make out of wet flour and cook on hot stones.

Even worse than the lack[10] of food is the lack of clothing. During that awful winter, those fortunate men who have blankets wear them all day. Some soldiers have no shoes, and they stand guard with their feet in their hats to keep them from freezing. One third of Washington's men are too sick to stand up. Another third run away. The situation seems hopeless, but their respect for George Washington and their love of liberty holds the army together.

Just in time, help comes from France which makes a large loan of money to the new country. A wealthy young French general, Lafayette, is partly responsible for arranging this help. He strongly supports the American

UCLA

George Washington

Revolution and comes to share the hardships of Valley Forge with General Washington. Lafayette serves in the American army and becomes a true hero, both in the United States and in France.

When spring comes, conditions get better. The army that General George Washington leads out of Valley Forge is an army to be proud of. By this time, powerful aid is coming from Spain and from Holland, as well as from France. And maybe even more important, France and Spain are at war with England and together they keep England busy defending herself in Europe. The Revolutionary War continues, and Americans slowly begin winning battles all the way from New York to Virginia. An army of simple American farm boys is beating King George's finest soldiers.

Lafayette by C.W. Peale

9 **reputation** — the opinion people have about someone
10 **lack** — not having any; not having enough

Washington crossing the Delaware River to surprise the British on Christmas

Chapter Four, Story Two
Washington At Valley Forge

Exercises

A. **Reading Comprehension — Discussion and Writing.** Choose one question to discuss with a partner. Write the answers to the rest, using your own words or copying them from the story.

1. Why does congress need money?

   _____

   _____

   _____

2. With all their troubles, how is George Washington able to keep his army together during the winter at Valley Forge?

   _____

   _____

   _____

3. What aid does America receive from other countries?

   _____

   _____

   _____

B. **Vocabulary.** Write a word, which you can find in the story, to complete each sentence.

1. George Washington has a good _____ as an officer.

2. While the British are staying comfortable in _____, Washington's army in Valley Forge lacks _____ and _____.

3. Help comes to America from the countries of _____, _____ and _____.

C. **Definitions.** Look up these words in your dictionary. Use each one in a sentence. Discuss the answers with your instructor.

1. aid

_____

_____

2. afford

_____

_____

3. firewood

_____

_____

4. respect

_____

_____

5. loan

_____

_____

6. hero

_____

_____

7. defend

_____

_____

Chapter Four, Story Three

The Constitution

On October 19, 1781, the British surrender[11] to General Washington. On April 19, 1783, just eight years after Paul Revere's famous ride, Great Britain and the United States of America sign a peace agreement. The American colonies are free from England forever.

The Revolutionary War is over, but the problems of the new country continue. Congress needs money and doesn't know how to get it. It can tax the states, as the colonies now call themselves, but they only pay when they want to. Each of the thirteen states acts like an independent country, with its own laws, its own constitution and, in some cases, its own money. It's hard for Europe to take seriously the weak government of the United States.

Alexander Hamilton, the brilliant[12] representative from New York, calls for a Constitutional Convention to meet in Philadelphia in 1787. The purpose of the convention is to write a constitution which can unite thirteen states into one nation.

Representatives begin to arrive. As they work, it becomes clear that the convention is deeply divided. Hamilton believes the United States must have a strong federal, or central, government. On his side are landowners, lawyers and business men. They do not trust[13] the common people to elect a president. They want the congress to choose a president to serve for life. On the other side are representatives who are for stronger states' rights. They remember King George very well, and they want a president without much power. Some of them don't want a president at all. They just intend to make sure that the new constitution protects, keeps safe, the rights of the people.

Of course, the problem of slavery comes up. The Southern states refuse to accept the constitution if it does not permit slavery to continue.

After months of discussion, the Constitutional Convention reaches a compromise. Under the constitution there is a president, and he does have great power — but he serves only four years at a time. The congress has two parts, called houses: one is the United States Senate, which has two senators for each state, no matter how big or small. The other is the House of Representatives, where the number of representatives depends on the population of each state. For that reason, the Southern states want to count their slaves as part of the population, and the Northern states don't want them to. Another compromise is reached. Each slave, whether man, woman or child, counts as three-fifths of a person.

By June 25, 1788, most of the states vote to accept the constitution. Soon after, there is an election. George Washington becomes the first president, and John Adams the first vice president, of the United States.

In 1789, because Thomas Jefferson insists[14], a Bill of Rights is added to the constitution. The Bill of Rights is the first ten amendments[15] to the constitution. Its purpose is to protect American citizens from their own government. It promises to the people, now and forever, freedom of speech, freedom of the press[16], freedom of religion, and other individual rights that are equally important.

Two hundred years later, through good times and bad times, the Constitution of the United States is still working.

[11] **surrender** — give up (to another person)
[12] **brilliant** — very intelligent
[13] **trust** — have faith
[14] **insist** — demand strongly
[15] **amendment** — repair, change
[16] **the press** — the newspapers

Chapter Four, Story Three
The Constitution

Exercises

A. **Reading Comprehension — Discussion and Writing.** Choose two questions to discuss with a partner. Write the answers to the rest, using your own words, or copying the answers from the story.

1. Why is it difficult for congress to get money from the states?

   _____

   _____

   _____

2. Why do Alexander Hamilton and others want a strong central government?

   _____

   _____

   _____

3. Why do other representatives want strong states' rights?

   _____

   _____

   _____

4. How do the two sides finally compromise under the constitution?

   _____

   _____

   _____

B. **Vocabulary.** Use the list of words below to fill in the blanks.

money   constitution   peace   agreement   laws

unite   states' rights   federal   central

1. In 1783, Britain and the United States end the Revolutionary War when they sign a _____. Each new state has its own _____, its own _____ and even its own _____. This makes it difficult for the new government to run a united country.

2. Many people want a strong _____ or _____ government, where congress chooses a president for life. Others want a weak government, with strong _____ and great protection of rights of the people.

3. Congress meets in Philadelphia in 1787 to write the constitution, to _____ the thirteen states.

C. **Definitions.** Fill in the blanks, using words from the story.

The constitution is a [1] _____ in which the laws of government are written.

At the Constitutional Convention, representatives from each side go half way in their arguments to agree, making many [2] _____, so that the separate states can unite as one [3] _____, one country.

The [4] _____ is the first ten amendments to the constitution which protects the individual rights of all Americans.

Chapter Five, Overview

Going West

George Washington serves two terms as president of the United States. He refuses to serve a third term and returns to private life in Virginia. John Adams, a hero of the American Revolution, is the second president, and Thomas Jefferson, the author[1] of the Declaration of Independence, is the third. Power passes from one president to the next smoothly and peacefully. The Constitution of the United States not only works, it works well.

The new country is growing fast. In 1803, the United States signs a treaty, or agreement, with France. It is known as the Louisiana Purchase. For $15,000,000, France sells to the United States a very large piece of land which becomes the states of Louisiana, Missouri, Arkansas, Iowa, Minnesota, Kansas, Oklahoma, Nebraska, North Dakota and South Dakota, most of Montana and Wyoming and part of Colorado, Texas and New Mexico.

The young United States is now more than twice as big as it was, but it has big problems too. In 1812, the United States and Great Britain fight another war. And, in 1846, the United States goes to war with Mexico. There are many causes for the Mexican war. One of them is that the United States wants to own all of what are now the states of Arizona, Texas, New Mexico and California, land which at this time belongs to Mexico. Meanwhile, millions and millions of acres[2] in the western part of the United States are quickly opening up for settlement.

The West! From the beginning of this country's history, Americans have always looked toward the setting sun where the land is rich. The newcomers are not thinking about who owns the land. They are thinking about owning it themselves. Many people living along the Atlantic Coast at this time cannot own land. It is expensive and taxes are high. There are others also, people who, for many reasons, need the opportunity the West offers. Like the first settlers, they want to escape to a new life. It is people like these who are looking for a new place in which to settle, to farm and build towns.

So thousands of them

A wagon train on the Oregon Trail

Library of Congress

United States in 1803

put their families, their tools and their furniture into wagons. They travel west, west into the great forests, west over great rivers and mountains, west into the endless grasslands. They travel in wagon trains of fifty to seventy-five wagons, one following the other — enough, they hope, to frighten away Indians who might attack a smaller group.

Soon, many of the trees in the forests are cut down. Soon, thousands of log cabins, houses made of tree logs, stand on Indian lands. The Indians fight hard to hold on to their land and their way of life, but it is a battle they cannot win.

Most of the time, the United States government protects the interests of its white citizens. The government makes agreements in writing with the Indians, or Native Americans, that it does not intend to keep. The Indians don't want to leave the land of their fathers and move into unknown country but they finally have to agree to go. In return[3], the government gives them new land, farther west, and promises that this land is theirs forever... "for as long as the sun shines or the waters run in the rivers," in the famous words of one of those agreements.

One after another, the agreements are broken, if not by congress, then by government officials and army officers without honor and without pity. The history of the American Indian in the eighteenth and nineteenth centuries is a history of broken promises.

[1] **author** — writer
[2] **acre** — a measure of land (43,560 square feet)
[3] **in return** — as something equal, in exchange

Chapter Five, Overview
Going West

Exercises

A. **Reading Comprehension — Discussion and Writing.** Choose two questions for discussion. Write the answers to the rest. You may look back in the story, or write the answers in your own words.

   1. How does the United States get land from France?

   _____

   _____

   _____

   2. How does the United States get land from Mexico?

   _____

   _____

   _____

   3. How do people from the Atlantic coast travel west?

   _____

   _____

   _____

   4. What agreements does the United States government make with Native Americans?

   _____

   _____

   _____

★ ★

B. **True or False?** Circle true or false. Write the sentences from the story that explain your answer.

1. True or false?

The Louisiana Purchase is an agreement to buy land from Mexico.

_____

_____

_____

2. True or false?

People travel west in large wagon trains because they enjoy being together.

_____

_____

_____

3. True or false?

The United States government makes the Indians move from their land, and agrees to give them other land, to keep forever.

_____

_____

_____

4. True or false?

The United States government keeps its agreements with the Indians.

_____

_____

_____

5. True or false?

The history of the American Indian in the 18th and 19th centuries is a history of broken promises.

_____

_____

_____

C. **Vocabulary.** Use these words to fill in the blanks in the sentences below.

honor   pity   grasslands   power   newcomers

1. They push west, into the endless _____.

2. Agreements are broken by government officials and army officers without _____ and without _____.

3. _____ passes from one president to the next smoothly and peacefully.

4. The _____ are not thinking about who owns the land.

Chapter Five, Story One

The Trail[4] of Tears

There is a popular saying in the United States in the nineteenth century: "The only good Indian is a dead Indian." Many white people feel that way. Indians hate the settlers who push them off their land, so they burn the whites' new houses, killing some women and children. Indians hunt and live on their land. They love it, but never think of it as something to own, unlike white men. The whites believe that Indians are savages, or wild people, like animals. They know nothing about God, so how can they have any rights to this good land? These are the excuses that white people use to kill them and to take away from these Native Americans the continent that was once theirs from ocean to ocean.

In the Tennessee River Valley, next to Georgia, lives the Cherokee Indian Nation. Unlike most Indian people, the Cherokees accept the white man's way of living. On their forty thousand square miles of rich land there are roads and schools and real houses, just like white people live in, and sometimes better. They have a constitution, and a senate, and a house of representatives. The Cherokees live so much like white men that they even have black slaves.

Many farmers in Georgia, whose land is not very good, look at that beautiful Cherokee land and want it for themselves. The government of Georgia decides to help them get it. Georgia influences the Congress of the United States to break an agreement which gives the Cherokees the right to own their land.

Instead of going to war, the Cherokee Nation takes its case to the Supreme Court. In 1832, John Ross, a Cherokee Chief who acts as a lawyer for his people, goes before the Supreme Court. He argues so intelligently that he wins the case.

It makes no difference[5]. Andrew Jackson, an old Indian fighter, is now the president of the United States and he is not sympathetic. Georgia government officials are able to find five hundred Cherokees who agree to sell the Tennessee Valley for a little bit of money and a few promises. Later, sixteen thousand Cherokees sign a paper telling the government in Washington that they do not want to sell their land. Again, it makes no difference. The president ignores it.

On May 2, 1838, seven thousand soldiers begin the unpleasant job of collecting all the Cherokee men, women and children into six hundred and forty-five wagons. They catch the Indians wherever they are, in their homes, at school, in the fields. At first, many try to run away, but they soon see that escape is impossible, and they go quietly, without hope.

So begins a journey of twelve hundred miles which the Cherokees call "The Trail of Tears." Four thousand Indians die on this long march, and their suffering is terrible to remember.

At last they cross the Mississippi River into Oklahoma, a new and strange land. Behind them lies their home, the land of their fathers and grandfathers, which they are never going to see again.

⁴ **trail** — a rough road, or path, across country
⁵ **it makes no difference** — it does not change anything

Trail of Tears

Chapter Five, Story One
Trail of Tears

Exercises

A. **Reading Comprehension — Discussion and Writing.** Choose two questions for discussion with a partner. Write the rest of the answers. You may look back at the story, or write answers in your own words.

1. Why do the Indians hate the white settlers?

   _____

   _____

   _____

2. In what ways do the Cherokee Indians live like white settlers?

   _____

   _____

   _____

3. How does the state of Georgia get the Indians' land in the Tennessee River Valley?

   _____

   _____

   _____

4. How do the soldiers make the Indians leave their land?

   _____

   _____

   _____

★ ★ ★ ★ ★ ★ ★ ★ ★ ★ ★ ★ ★ ★ ★ ★ ★ ★ ★ ★

B. Choose the best answer for these sentences:

1. The Indians

   a. push the white settlers off their land.

   b. don't know what to do with the land.

   c. don't think of owning the land.

2. The Cherokees fight to keep their land and

   a. go to war with the United States.

   b. take their case to the Supreme Court.

   c. build their homes and schools like the white settlers.

3. The president, Andrew Jackson,

   a. is not sympathetic.

   b. wins the case for the Cherokees in the Supreme Court.

   c. crosses the Mississippi River into Oklahoma.

C. **Definitions.** Draw a line between words on the left and words on the right that have nearly the same meaning.

1. warning   a. to be in agreement, in feeling

2. settlers   b. telling about something, usually bad or dangerous, before it happens

3. excuse   c. to bring together

4. sympathetic   d. explanation, or reason

5. collect   e. people who come to stay in a new country

Chapter Five, Story Two

The Forty-Niners

On May 12, 1846, Congress declares war against Mexico. Many Americans criticize the government for doing this. Still, the war continues. In September, 1847, the United States army attacks Mexico City. The Mexicans fight bravely, but in the end the United States wins the war. In the Peace Treaty of 1848, it wins also all of Texas, Arizona, New Mexico and California.

A few months later, gold is discovered near the American River in northern California. News of this discovery travels fast. At this time, San Francisco is just a village, with a population of about eight hundred. When the news of gold gets there, most of the eight hundred run off to the American River. The few streets of San Francisco are quiet and empty.

It takes longer for the excitement to reach the East. In December, 1848, 20 ounces of pure gold from California arrive in Washington, D.C. The newspapers go wild. Everyone goes wild. The great California Gold Rush begins.

Eighty-five thousand people who think they are going to find gold and be rich forever leave for California in 1849. They come from every part of the United States, from Mexico, even from Europe and Asia. These are the famous "forty-niners."

There are three ways to get to California from the eastern United States. The most comfortable way is to go by ship around the tip of South America, and then north to San Francisco. The problem is that it takes between four and eight months to complete the journey. By the time the passengers arrive, there isn't going to be much gold left for them to find. Even so, 549 ships arrive in San Francisco from the East Coast in 1849. The minute they touch land, the passengers, the sailors and the captains run off to look for gold.

A faster way to get to California is to cross Central America where the distance between the Atlantic and the Pacific Oceans is shortest, and then continue north by boat. The forty-niners who come that way can expect bad food, bad water, disease, and the possibility that the boat may never come to pick them up.

A third way is to cross the country by land, in covered wagons. This way is slow and dangerous. Some wagon trains suffer terribly, both from freezing winter weather and from Indian attacks.

When the forty-niners finally reach California, they find that life is very hard. Because of the Gold Rush, everything is expensive. The few hotels are so crowded that there are often ten or more men sleeping in the same room. In the mining towns, crime is common. To protect themselves, the miners[6] organize their own governments. For criminals there is quick, rough justice: a rope and a tree.

California gold diggers — a scene from life at the mines

Most of the forty-niners find little gold, if any. Some of them go on to other parts of the West and try to get lucky there. Those who stay in California look for different ways to make a living. The Gold Rush is over, but as a result of the Gold Rush, the population of California grows from ten thousand to almost a hundred thousand in four years.

[6] **miners** — people who dig from the earth.

Chapter Five, Story Two
The Forty-Niners

Exercises

A. **Reading Comprehension — Discussion and Writing.** Choose two questions for discussion with a partner. Write the rest. You may look back and copy your answers from the story, or write them in your own words.

1. What do the people do there, when gold is discovered in northern California?

_____

_____

_____

2. How can people from eastern United States get to California?

_____

_____

_____

3. Why is everything expensive in California during the Gold Rush?

_____

_____

_____

4. How does California change after the Gold Rush?

_____

_____

_____

B. Choose the best answers for these sentences:

1. Congress declares war on Mexico because

    a. it wants the gold in California.

    b. the Mexican army attacks the United States.

    c. it wants the land of Texas, Arizona, New Mexico and California.

2. Life in California during the Gold Rush is

    a. difficult, because everything is expensive.

    b. comfortable, because people find a lot of gold.

    c. well organized, because the miners set up their own government.

Slavery

The problem of slavery in the United States is older than the country itself. At the time of the American Revolution, slavery does not exist in England, but trade in slaves with the colonies is still active until 1811.

Slave ships, some of them British and some owned by Northern merchants[1], arrive from Africa bringing angry, frightened blacks to the slave markets of America. The slaves are packed into the ships so tightly that many of them die before the journey is over. Sharks often follow these ships, waiting for bodies to be thrown into the sea.

Soon after the Revolution, it becomes clear that the Northern states have no real use for slaves. In the North, there are many factories, but most farms are small. In the South, large farms grow big money crops[2] like tobacco, rice and cotton. Slaves who can work long hours in the hot sun are a great advantage. Crops need to be picked on time, and slaves don't go on strike[3].

They become even more important to the South when Eli Whitney invents the cotton gin in 1793. This machine makes it possible for the first time to separate the cotton quickly from its seed. Without the machine, this is a very slow job. Because of the cotton gin, much more cotton is planted and must be picked by hand. The South is soon selling a million tons of cotton a year to the countries of Europe.

There are by this time four million blacks in the United States, but not many more are coming in. Most of them work in the cotton fields. They now must work harder than ever before. Many slave owners do not even live on their farms, which are run by cruel overseers, or managers. However, slave owners who are getting rich from slavery have no desire to give it up.

There are other people, mostly in the North, but some also in the South, who feel slavery is wrong and must not continue. These people are called abolitionists because they want to abolish, or put an end to slavery. Abolitionists make it their business to let the public know how cruel slavery is, how it tears mothers away from children, and husbands from their wives. In 1852, the cause[5] of abolition is helped by Harriet Beecher Stowe, a white woman, who writes a book called "Uncle Tom's Cabin." This story, about the suffering of the slaves, brings tears to the eyes of people all over the world. The book sells hundreds of thousands of copies, and it influences many people to support abolition.

In 1854, Congress passes the Kansas Nebraska Act. This law says that people who live in any new state may vote to decide whether or not to allow slavery in that state. At this very time, territories[4] of California, Texas, Kansas and Nebraska are hurrying to become part of the Union, as the United States is often called. The South wants to make sure that the new states permit slaves. The North wants to make sure they do not.

In 1857, the famous Dred Scott decision of the United States Supreme Court helps the cause of those Southerners who support slavery. Dred Scott is a slave. His master takes him north to live in Illinois. Since Illinois is a free state and does not allow slavery, Scott goes to court to demand his freedom. The opinion of the Court is that a slave is property, not a citizen, and that slave owners have the right to take their property anywhere they wish.

The struggles between the North and the South are becoming more and more bitter. There is reason to fear that they may destroy the Union.

1 **merchants** — people who buy and sell something
2 **crop** — what grows in the ground, like tobacco, rice and cotton
3 **strike** — to refuse to work until certain demands by the workers are met
4 **territory** — part of the country which is not a state, but which has an appointed governor
5 **cause** — any important subject that a group of people support

Slaves in the cotton fields of Georgia

Library of Congress

Chapter Six, Overview
Slavery

Exercises

A. **Reading Comprehension — Discussion and Writing.** Choose three questions to discuss with a partner. Write answers to the rest, looking back at the story, or using your own words.

1. How do the slaves come to America?

_____

_____

_____

2. How important are slaves to the North after the Revolution?

_____

_____

_____

3. How important are slaves to the South after the Revolution?

_____

_____

_____

4. How do most Southern slave owners feel about slavery?

_____

_____

_____

5. Who are the abolitionists?

_____

_____

_____

6. Why is the Kansas Nebraska Act important to both the North and the South?

_____

_____

_____

B. **True Or False.** Circle true or false. Write sentences from the story to explain your answer.

1. True or false?

   In the North, slaves are very important as farm workers.

   _____

   _____

   _____

2. True or false?

   The Kansas Nebraska Act is a law that says a new state coming into the Union allows slavery.

   _____

   _____

   _____

★ ★

3. True or false?

Abolitionists want to put an end to slavery.

_____

_____

_____

4. True or false?

The Court frees Dred Scott from slavery because he lives in the free state of Illinois.

_____

_____

_____

C. **Vocabulary.** Fill in the blanks with words you remember from your reading.

1. Eli Whitney's cotton gin makes it possible to quickly separate the

   a._____ from its b._____.

2. Harriet Beecher Stowe writes a book about the c._____ of the slaves. It influences many people to support d._____.

Chapter Six, Story One

Harriet Tubman and the Underground Railroad

People who try to defend slavery say that the slaves are happy. They sing and dance like children, and they love their masters. If that is true, it is hard to understand why so many of them escape and run away to the North at the first chance.

Freedom for many runaway slaves becomes possible through an organization called the Underground Railroad. It is run mostly by abolitionists, free blacks and escaped slaves. These brave "conductors," as they are called, lead the runaway slaves, secretly and usually at night, from one "station" of the Underground Railroad to the next. The stations are often the homes of friendly white people who are willing to hide the escaping slaves for a few days. The runaways are in great danger. If the slave-hunters catch them, they may be sent back to the South in chains. Punishment may include being sold to another master who is so far away that the slave will never see his family again.

One of the most famous conductors on the Underground Railroad is a short black woman named Harriet Tubman. Harriet is born in 1820 on a Maryland farm. Her mother, father, brothers and sisters are all slaves owned by their master, Edward Brodas. Brodas is not a very successful farmer. He makes his money by letting poor farmers, who cannot buy slaves of their own, pay him to use his.

When Harriet is seven years old, her master sends her to live with Miss Susan, a white woman who pays Brodas a few cents a week to hire the little black girl. One of Harriet's jobs is to keep Miss Susan's baby from crying. If Harriet can't keep the baby quiet, Miss Susan beats her. Once, Harriet runs away and hides with the pigs, eating their food for three or four days. Miss Susan decides she doesn't want Harriet any more and sends her back home.

Harriet goes to work in the fields. She cuts down trees, chops wood, does a man's work and grows as strong as a man. She can't read or write, but she is learning other important things. She learns that if you follow the North Star in the night sky it will lead you to the Northern States, to freedom. When Edward Brodas dies, Harriet gets a new master. She hears that he is going to sell her and decides that it is time for her to follow the North Star. With the help of the Underground Railroad, Harriet Tubman arrives safely in the free state of Pennsylvania.

How wonderful freedom is! Harriet gets a job and discovers that she can keep all the money she earns. It is hers. But she can't be happy because her brothers and sisters are still in slavery. Now that she knows the way, she decides to go back and lead them out, too. She does, and then she goes right back and leads out some other slaves.

In the years that follow, Harriet Tubman returns to Maryland nineteen times. She takes more than three hundred slaves north to freedom. Wherever they may be, slaves know about this brave black woman. They tell their children that someday, maybe, she will come for them. The slave owners know about her too, and they offer a reward of $60,000 to anyone who can catch her. Nobody ever does.

There are many interesting stories about Harriet Tubman. One night she is leading some escaping

Harriet Tubman

slaves through a dark wood. One of them becomes frightened and wants to turn back. Harriet knows it is too dangerous to let this man go home. His master may make him tell what he knows about the Underground Railroad. Harriet pulls a gun out of her pocket and points it at him.

"You go on," she says, "or you die."

The man does not hesitate long. He goes on.

Chapter Six, Story One
Harriet Tubman and the Underground Railroad

Exercises

A. **Reading Comprehension — Discussion and Writing.** Choose two questions to discuss with a partner. Write the rest of the answers, looking at the story, or using your own words.

1. Who runs the Underground Railroad?

   _____

   _____

   _____

2. Who is Harriet Tubman?

   _____

   _____

   _____

3. What does Harriet learn that helps her escape to the free Northern states?

   _____

   _____

   _____

4. What does Harriet do to free other slaves?

   _____

   _____

   _____

★ ★ ★ ★ ★ ★ ★ ★ ★ ★ ★ ★ ★ ★ ★ ★ ★ ★ ★ ★

B. Vocabulary. Fill in the correct word from the story.

Abolitionists who run the Underground Railroad are called [a.]_____

They hide runaway slaves in [b.]_____ along the way to the North.

Slave owners who know about Harriet Tubman offer a [c.]_____ to any-one who catches her.

Chapter Six, Story Two

John Brown at Harper's Ferry

Another conductor on the Underground Railroad is a white man, a tall man with a straight back and clear, gray eyes. John Brown is his name, and America is going to remember it always.

John Brown's father is very religious. He teaches his children to love God and hate slavery. When John Brown has children of his own, he teaches them in exactly the same way. Brown has seven children with his first wife, thirteen with his second. Life in the new western land of Ohio is difficult. Of Brown's twenty children, only eleven live to grow up.

Like his father, John Brown raises sheep. He works hard and makes a good living. But he continues to do everything he can to abolish slavery in America. When he builds a new barn[6] he makes sure there is a secret room in it where escaping slaves can hide on their way to Canada.

"I have no better use for my life than to lay it down in the cause of the slave," says John Brown.

In 1854, Brown's oldest sons decide to get land in Kansas, which is soon to become a new state. As a result of the Kansas Nebraska Act, thousands of people on both sides of the slavery question rush to settle in Kansas and vote. Slave owners can't travel easily with their slaves, so they hire men to travel ahead to Kansas and vote for them. These are rough, tough people, and they ride into Kansas on their horses, shooting their guns and trying to frighten others into voting for slavery. They kill some of the abolitionists.

John Brown's sons ask their father to come to Kansas. When he does, he brings with him guns, gunpowder and a plan for action. He wants to punish those who are responsible for killing abolitionists. He kills five people who he believes support slavery. He intends to do whatever is necessary to free the slaves, as many as he can. He hopes that thousands of them will join him and follow him to freedom.

"Talk does not free the slaves," says John Brown.

On October 16, 1859, John Brown, age sixty, rides with twenty-one younger men into the little town of

UCLA

John Brown

Harper's Ferry, Virginia. With Brown are five blacks and sixteen whites, including his sons, Owen, Watson and Oliver. There is a building at Harper's Ferry where the federal[7] government keeps guns. Brown's people capture that building, take the guns, kill some men and take many prisoners. The next morning, John Brown is still there. Instead of escaping while he can, the old man waits. What is he waiting for? Perhaps he is waiting for those thousands of slaves and abolitionists to come join him. They don't come, but the United States Marines do. Watson Brown, Oliver Brown and eight others die in the fighting. John Brown himself is seriously hurt and he finally surren-

U.S. Marines storming engine house at Harper's Ferry

John Brown is taken to prison after his trial

ders. His trial, for murder and treason[8] against the state of Virginia, is very quick. On December 2, 1859, he and six of his young men die by hanging.

John Brown lives on in history. To some, he is just a criminal, a mentally sick killer. Many others, from that time to the present, remember him as a hero, a martyr[9], a man with the will to fight a great evil[10] and the courage to die for what he believes is right.

[6] **barn** — a large farm building used for storing crops, or for farm animals.
[7] **federal** — central government of United States.
[8] **treason** — acting against a person's own government.
[9] **martyr** — a person killed because of what he or she believes.
[10] **evil** — bad or wrong.

Chapter Six, Story Two
John Brown at Harper's Ferry

Exercises

A. Reading Comprehension — Discussion and Writing. Choose two questions to discuss with a partner. Write answers to the rest, looking back at the story, or using your own words.

1. What things does John Brown do to support abolition?

   _____

   _____

   _____

2. What does John Brown do at Harper's Ferry, Virigina?

   _____

   _____

   _____

3. How does John Brown pay for what he believes?

   _____

   _____

   _____

B. Vocabulary. Fill in the words from the story to complete the sentence.

1. John Brown hides [a.]_____ slaves in a [b.]_____ [c.]_____

   in his barn.

2. John Brown kills five people in Kansas as [a.]_____ for killing some

   [b.]_____.

3. John Brown and his men capture a building that belongs to the [a.]_____

   [b.]_____.

4. They take [a.]_____, kill some men, and take many [b.]_____.

5. His trial, for [a.]_____ and [b.]_____ is very quick.

6. To some people, he is just a [a.]_____. Others remember him as a

   [b.]_____ and a [c.]_____.

Chapter Seven, Overview

The Civil War

From the time of President Jefferson, the Democratic Party is the most important political party in the new United States. In the election of 1860, a new party, the Republican Party, chooses a lawyer from a small town in Illinois to be its candidate for president. This candidate does not have much experience in government but he seems to understand and represent the feelings of the people in the Northern States. His name is Abraham Lincoln.

The Republicans, who are trying to prevent slavery from spreading to the new states, win the election by a very few votes. The fact that Abe Lincoln, a Republican, is going to move into the White House angers the South. Southerners remember Lincoln saying, "I believe this government cannot endure permanently half slave and half free."

Lincoln's purpose is to save the Union, not to either save or destroy slavery. His election is a signal for the Southern states to secede from, to declare they are no longer part of, the United States. The seceding states form their own government, the Confederate States of America. Jefferson Davis becomes their president. He and most white people in the South now believe they are strong enough to win the war which everybody knows is coming.

On April 12, 1861, at 4:30 in the morning, the Confederates fire the first gun of the Civil War. They attack Fort Sumter, in South Carolina, a fort which belongs to the United States government.

So begins the long, terrible Civil War that results in the death of six hundred thousand Union and Confederate soldiers. Before it is over, the American land is red with the blood of its sons.

The South has the advantage of fighting on its own ground to defend the Southern way of life. The South, especially with its famous General Robert E. Lee, has much better generals than the North. The North has greater wealth, greater population, more factories, more railroads. That becomes important later, but for a long time it looks as if those smart Confederate officers on their fast horses may win the war for the South.

Lincoln is unsure of himself at first, but grows to become a powerful leader. When it seems politically necessary, Lincoln writes the famous Emancipation Proclamation which frees the slaves in states now at war with the Union. At first, the Union Army does not accept blacks and sometimes even sends escaping slaves back to their masters. But after the Emancipation Proclamation, more than two hundred thousand blacks fight for the North. They now certainly have great reason to fight. Sixty thousand of them give up their lives for the Union.

The war goes on. And on. President Lincoln is disappointed in some of his generals who are afraid of General Lee and who avoid meeting him on the battlefield. He finally finds a general, Ulysses S. Grant, who has the will to fight. Slowly, the North begins winning important battles. By this time, Southerners are poor, hungry and tired. Their land is in ruins, their cities are burning.

On April 9, 1865, General Lee surrenders to General Grant. After so much suffering on both sides, the Civil War is over. The slaves are at last free and the Union is safe.

After the war, the South begins to reconstruct, or rebuild, itself. During the Reconstruction Period, there is a struggle between those who want to give the newly free slaves the right to vote, and those who want to keep black people powerless: free, but not equal. The Fourteenth Amendment, which becomes part of the constitution at this time, requires the states to allow "all adult male citizens" to vote. The amendment makes it clear that, while adult black men may possibly be given the vote, adult women of any color will certainly not. This comes as a deep disappointment to many American women who, in the last half of the nineteenth century, are beginning to organize and speak out in public for their rights, especially the right to vote.

It is not until 1919 that the Nineteenth Amendment to the Constitution, Woman Suffrage[1], is passed into law. It says that in all ways, under the law, women have the same rights as men.

---

[1] **Suffrage** — the right to vote

★ ★

Chapter Seven, Overview
The Civil War

Exercises

A. **Reading Comprehension — Discussion and Writing.** Choose three questions to discuss with a partner. Write the rest, looking back at the story, or using your own words.

1. Why does the new Republican Party choose Abraham Lincoln for its candidate in 1860?

_____

_____

_____

2. Why do the Southern states secede from the Union?

_____

_____

_____

3. What does the Emancipation Proclamation do for the blacks?

_____

_____

_____

4. What is the struggle during the Reconstruction period that affects the newly freed slaves?

_____

_____

_____

5. What is the Fourteenth Amendment?

_____

_____

_____

6. What new law regarding women is passed in 1919?

_____

_____

_____

B. Choose the correct answer for these sentences:

1. The new Republican Party of 1860 chooses Abraham Lincoln because

   a. his purpose is to destroy slavery.

   b. he understands the feelings of the people of the North.

   c. he wants to save the Union.

2. The Southern states secede from the Union because

   a. they have better generals than the North.

   b. they want to continue slavery.

   c. Lincoln writes the Emancipation Proclamation.

3. The Emancipation Proclamation

   a. frees the South to defend the Southern way of life.

   b. frees slaves in states at war with the Union.

   c. frees slaves to fight for the North.

4. The Fourteenth Amendment to the United States Constitution allows

   a. adult male citizens to vote.

   b. black women to vote.

   c. adult women of any color to vote.

★ ★ ★ ★ ★ ★ ★ ★ ★ ★ ★ ★ ★ ★ ★ ★ ★ ★ ★ ★

C. **Complete the Sentences.** Draw a line from the words on the left to the words on the right to complete the sentences.

1. The new Republican Party　　　　　a. surrenders to General Ulysses S. Grant.

2. Jefferson Davis　　　　　　　　　　b. wants to prevent slavery from spreading to the new states.

3. In the Civil War　　　　　　　　　　c. many thousands of Americans die, from both the North and the South.

4. The Emancipation Proclamation　　d. frees slaves in states at war with the Union.

5. At the end of the Civil War,　　　　e. becomes president of the Confederate General Robert E. Lee　　　　　　　　States.

Chapter Seven, Story

Abraham Lincoln (Part One)

When Abraham Lincoln is born, on February 12, 1809, the population of the whole United States is only seven million. Thomas Jefferson is still alive. The Indians are still fighting back. The great Southwest, which includes Texas and California, still belongs to Mexico

Kentucky, where Lincoln is born, is a slave state, but the Lincolns don't own any slaves. They don't own much of anything. Lincoln's father is a poor man who struggles to make a living. Neither of Lincoln's parents knows how to read or write. The log cabin where Lincoln is born has one room, one door, and one window. As a child, Lincoln sometimes goes to school, but only when his father doesn't need him. The boy learns to read by reading the Bible and those few books he can borrow. He reads them over and over again.

The Lincolns move to Indiana. Eight year old Abraham, already tall for his age and dressed in pants made of deerskin and a raccoon hat, walks with his family every step of the one hundred miles. In Indiana, Abe helps his father cut down trees to clear the land. He helps him plant corn and pumpkins. When his mother dies, Abe helps his father bury her.

In 1831, Lincoln decides it is time to move on. He is now twenty-two years old, six feet, four inches tall, thin, but very strong. Nobody can say he is handsome, but he has a face that people do not forget. He moves to New Salem, Illinois (population, one hundred) and gets a job in the general store. He likes to talk to people, tell jokes, discuss political issues. After a while, young Lincoln gets the idea that he ought to go into politics. He runs for election to the state legislature. He loses, but people in Illinois begin to pay attention to him.

Lincoln decides he wants to be a lawyer. At this time there are no law schools. Young men who want to practice law read

Library of Congress

Log cabin like Abraham Lincoln's birthplace

law books in the offices of practicing lawyers until they are ready to take their examinations. Lincoln does it differently. He reads those big, heavy law books all by himself, passes his examinations and opens a law office in Springfield, Illinois.

Springfield, with a population of two thousand, seems to Lincoln to be a busy, exciting town. He meets some interesting people there. One of them is Stephen A. Douglas, who is becoming an important man in the Democratic Party. Another is a small young woman from a rich Southern family who is visiting her sister in Springfield. Her name is Mary Todd.

Abe Lincoln and Mary fall in love. To the Todds, Lincoln seems to be a man with no money and few manners, not a proper husband for an expensively educated girl like Mary. Lincoln tries to forget her. He is angry with her family.

"One 'd' is enough for God," he tells a friend bitterly, "but the Todds need two."

In the end, the Todd family accepts Lincoln as a son-in-law and helps him buy the Springfield house in which he and Mary and their sons live until they move to the White House in Washington, D.C.

In 1846, Lincoln, still interested in politics, is elected to the U.S. House of Representatives. There he speaks so strongly against the Mexican War that the Illinois voters, who support the war, do not elect him again. Back to Springfield he goes to continue his successful law practice. He never forgets that, in the new and still unfinished capital of the United States of America, there are slave markets whose business it is to sell human beings. Abraham Lincoln is not an abolitionist, but the problem of slavery troubles him more and more.

Chapter Seven, Story
Abraham Lincoln (Part One)

Exercises

A. **Reading Comprehension — Discussion and Writing.** Choose two questions to discuss with a partner. Write the rest, looking back at the story, or using your own words.

1. How does Abraham Lincoln get his education as a child?

_____

_____

_____

2. How does Lincoln become a lawyer?

_____

_____

_____

3. Why does Lincoln not get elected to the House of Representatives for the second time?

_____

_____

_____

B. **Vocabulary.** Choose a word from the list below to complete these sentences.

Mexican War   clear   son-in-law   political   slave   law

1. Kentucky, where Lincoln is born, is a _____ state.

2. He helps his father cut down trees to _____ the land.

3. Lincoln enjoys discussing _____ issues.

4. By reading _____ books by himself, he passes his examination.

5. Mary Todd's family finally accepts Lincoln as a _____.

6. Lincoln loses the second election to the House of Representatives in Illinois because he speaks out against the _____.

Abraham Lincoln (Part Two)

Stephen A. Douglas, now a powerful U.S. Senator, supports the Kansas Nebraska Act of 1854. This law says that people who live in any new state may vote to decide whether or not to allow slavery in that state. It is this Act of Congress which causes so much trouble in Kansas and which at last makes Abraham Lincoln stand up and speak out against slavery. A new political party is born, the Republican Party. Republicans oppose slavery for the new territories.

Lincoln becomes a Republican and, in 1856, runs against the Democrat, Douglas, for the Senate. The two candidates, Lincoln very tall, Douglas very short, meet seven times in the famous Lincoln-Douglas debates. They argue face to face. Lincoln argues for protecting the Union, and for keeping slavery out of the new territories. Newspaper reporters travel to the debates from all over the nation. Lincoln loses the election to Douglas, but he does so well in the debates that important Republicans begin to notice him.

In 1860, the Republicans need a strong candidate to run for president against Douglas, the candidate of the Democratic Party. They choose Lincoln. It is a narrow victory but the Republicans win the election. Abraham Lincoln, the sixteenth president of the United States, takes his wife and his children to Washington, D.C.

The Civil War begins soon after. There are photographs (for the camera is just beginning to be used) which show old and

Abraham Lincoln

Library of Congress

tired Mr. Lincoln becomes in just four short years. The newspapers make fun of his appearance. The abolitionists attack him for moving too slowly against slavery. Some Democrats attack him because he does not try to make peace with the Confederate States. Meanwhile, the cost of the war, in lives and in money, keeps growing.

At Gettysburg, Pennsylvania, one hundred and seventy thousand Union and Confederate troops fight the bloodiest battle of the war. The Union forces win. Some of the seven thousand dead are still not buried when the president arrives to speak on the recent battlefield. He speaks for only two minutes, but many people believe that Lincoln's Gettysburg Address, as it is known, is one of the great speeches of all time. In it, he talks of his great sorrow, both for the war and for its necessity. He says that the world will never forget these soldiers who died to give the country "a new birth of freedom." He promises that "government of the people, by the people, and for the people, shall not perish[2] from the earth."

Before the next presidential election of 1864, it becomes clear that the North is winning the war. Lincoln wins his second term by a great many votes. On April 9, 1865, Confederate General Robert E. Lee surrenders to the Union's General Ulysses S. Grant and the war ends.

General Grant does not make prisoners of the defeated Confederate soldiers. He takes away their guns, but he allows them to keep their horses so they may return to their farms, to work, and to reconstruct their lives and their cities. It is a very sad victory.

On the night of April 14, 1865 President and Mrs. Lincoln, smiling and happy, go to a theater in Washington to see a comedy. John Wilkes Booth, an actor and a strong supporter of the Confederate cause, goes behind the President's chair and shoots him in the head. Abraham Lincoln dies the next morning.

A week later, a funeral train carries Lincoln's body home to Springfield, Illinois. For all those sixteen hundred miles, people wait near the railroad tracks — thousands of them, black and white. Some of them wait for days. They just want to say good-bye.

[2]   **perish** — die

Chapter Seven, Story
Abraham Lincoln (Part Two)

Exercises

A. **Reading Comprehension — Discussion and Writing.** Choose three questions to discuss with a partner. Write the rest, looking back at the story, or using your own words.

1. What is the important issue of the new Republican Party?

_____

_____

_____

2. What are some of Lincoln's arguments in the Lincoln-Douglas debates?

_____

_____

_____

3. How do abolitionists feel about Lincoln after the Civil War?

_____

_____

_____

4. What is the terrible cost of the Civil War?

_____

_____

_____

5. What do Lincoln's words, "government of the people, by the people, for the people" mean?

_____

_____

_____

6. What do the people do when Lincoln is killed?

_____

_____

_____

B. **True or False?** Circle true or false. Write a sentence from the story to support your answer.

1. True or false? Stephen A. Douglas thinks the new territories need to decide for themselves whether or not to allow slavery.

_____

_____

_____

2. True or false? Lincoln, the Republican candidate, does not support slavery in the new territories.

_____

_____

_____

3. True or false? The Confederate States leave the Union after Lincoln is elected.

_____

_____

_____

4. True or false? Lincoln feels a great sorrow that the soldiers who died in the war are going to be forgotten.

_____

_____

_____

5. True or false? General Grant takes many Confederate prisoners when the war ends.

_____

_____

_____

6. True or false? The country is once again united, and everyone returns home satisfied.

_____

_____

_____

Chapter Eight, Overview

The Age of Industry and Invention

Between the years 1850 and 1900, the United States races full speed ahead into the age of industry and invention.

Work that has always been done by sweat and muscle is now done by steam and electricity. In agriculture, or farming, labor-saving farm machinery changes the way America grows its food. It is no longer economically[1] practical for a farmer to grow everything his family needs on his own small farm. Small farms are replaced[2] by big farms which, with the help of big machines, usually grow one large crop.

In industry, a new product, steel, replaces iron. Railroads cross the land from the Atlantic

Inventor Thomas A. Edison holding a model of the electric lamp

Library of Congress

to the Pacific. Suddenly there are factories almost everywhere and in them, for the first time, thousands of women find regular work outside the home. In Pennsylvania and in Texas wells dig deep into the earth to bring up oil. Oil makes the wheels of all the new machines turn smoothly and lights the lamps of the entire world.

Industry develops at a speed that is unbelievable.

In 1858, George M. Pullman builds the first railroad sleeping car. In the same year, after many disappointments, a cable[3] is laid on the bottom of the sea between the United States and England. Now Europe and America are connected by telegraph[4].

In 1868, the Otis brothers open a factory where they manufacture elevators which make it possible for buildings in crowded cities to be taller and taller.

In 1874, the first practical typewriter (with only capital letters) is put on the market.

In 1875, the first refrigerated railroad car delivers meat safely to far parts of the country.

In 1876, Alexander Graham Bell invents the telephone.

In 1878, Thomas Alva Edison invents the phonograph, and a year later, he invents the electric light bulb.

By 1900, there are almost eight thousand privately owned automobiles in the United States.

All these important inventions change the way Americans live, work, farm, and conduct business. The new wealth that results from so much industrial progress also creates new problems. Some leaders of industry use their wealth to improve life for everyone. But there are others who use their money and power only for the purpose of getting more money and more power. These Robber Barons, as they are called, buy Congressmen's votes as easily as they buy corporations[5], and a whole lot cheaper. They care nothing for the land they ruin as they develop new mines and build new railroads, and they care nothing for the working people who dig the coal, lay the railroad tracks and operate the machines.

To defend themselves, the workers organize unions. By 1870 there are national unions representing steelworkers, clothing workers, bricklayers and about thirty other trades. The purpose of these unions is to protect the jobs of their members and to get higher pay and better working conditions for them. Sometimes the unions call strikes in which the workers refuse to work until their employers agree to their demands. The employers fight back by hiring strike breakers. Strike breakers are new workers the employers hire to do the jobs of the striking workers. Violence often results.

Meanwhile, in Washington D.C., the government of President McKinley, which sympathizes with Cuba in its fight for independence from Spain, is getting ready to declare war against Spain.

That is the situation in America as the nineteenth century ends and the twentieth century is born.

[1] **economically** — regarding the spending of money
[2] **replace** — take the place of
[3] **cable** — a thick heavy bunch of wires that electricity can pass through
[4] **telegraph** — a system for sending messages by electricity
[5] **corporation** — a business which many people, together, own

★ ★

Chapter Eight, Overview
The Age of Industry and Invention

Exercises

A. **Reading Comprehension — Discussion and Writing.** Choose two questions to discuss with a partner. Write the rest, looking back at the story, or using your own words.

1. What are some of the new inventions that improve life in the United States between 1850 and 1900 ?

   _____

   _____

   _____

2. How does industrial progress create new problems for the land and for working people?

   _____

   _____

   _____

3. What do workers do to protect their jobs?

   _____

   _____

   _____

4. How do employers fight their striking workers?

   _____

   _____

   _____

B. **Definitions.** Draw a line from a word on the left to a word or phrase on the right with a similar meaning.

1. practical   a. create

2. invent   b. holes deep underground

3. wells   c. business

4. union   d. useful

5. industry   e. labor organization

Chapter Eight, Story One

Mr. Singer's Sewing Machine

By 1851, there are at least half a dozen men who claim that they are the inventors of the sewing machine. Several of these are already manufacturing and selling sewing machines before Isaac Merrit Singer even begins thinking about them. The trouble is, none of the early sewing machines works very well. They seem like expensive toys and people don't take them seriously.

Isaac Singer runs away from home before he is twelve years old, does a lot of traveling, and becomes an excellent mechanic. But that isn't what he wants to do. He wants to be an actor. Though he can hardly read, he learns a few parts from plays by Shakespeare and joins a theater company. It is only when he really needs some money that he takes a job in a mechanic's shop for a while.

In 1851, Singer is working for a mechanic named Orson Phelps in Boston when a disgusted owner brings her sewing machine into the shop to be fixed. Singer examines the machine and explains to Phelps exactly why it doesn't work and how to correct it. Phelps is interested. If Singer understands how to build a sewing machine that actually sews, the two of them can make a fortune.

A third man, George Zieber, also wants to make a fortune. He gives the other two men forty dollars to pay for the cost of developing a new, practical sewing machine.

It takes Singer eleven days to make a sewing machine that, for the first time, does continuous stitching[6]. Singer, Phelps and Zieber immediately go into business as I.M.Singer & Co., and start manufacturing sewing machines. Almost at once, Elias Howe, the inventor of an earlier sewing machine, takes them to court and demands $25,000 as punishment for using his ideas. This is the beginning of the "sewing machine wars." All the manufacturers of sewing machines and their lawyers fight each other in the courts for years.

All this time, I.M. Singer is making and selling his sewing machines just as fast as he can. When the "sewing machine wars" are finally over, Singer's sewing machines are so well known that everybody wants to own one.

One of the reasons for the unbelievable success of the Singer sewing machine is the company's introduction of installment plan selling. This means that people who want to buy a sewing machine do not have to pay for it all at one time but can pay over a long period, in installments. The idea of installment plan selling influences the development of business in the United States. Many other businesses begin to use the installment plan to make it easier to sell their products.

The sewing machine changes the way life is lived not only in America, but everywhere. It takes fourteen hours and twenty minutes of hand work to sew a man's shirt. By the time of the Civil War, a shirt can be made on a sewing machine in a little over an hour. The Union Army hires workers, most of them women, to sew uniforms on the the new machines. More than any other invention, the sewing machine changes the position of women in society. It takes millions of them out of the home, off the farm, and into industry.

Isaac Singer, meanwhile, gets tired of manufacturing sewing machines. He is now a very, very wealthy man and he builds himself a house in France. The house has one hundred and fifteen rooms, so there is lots of space when one or more of his twenty-four children comes to visit.

[5] **stitching** — sewing

I.M. Singer and Company at 458 Broadway, New York City

★ ★

Chapter 8, Story One,
Mr. Singer's Sewing Machine

Exercises

A. **Reading Comprehension — Discussion and Writing.** Choose two questions to discuss with a partner. Write the rest, looking back at the story, or using your own words.

1. How does Isaac Singer go into the sewing machine business?

   _____

   _____

   _____

2. What is the installment plan, and how does it work?

   _____

   _____

   _____

3. Why does the installment plan make it easier to sell things?

   _____

   _____

   _____

4. How does the sewing machine change life for women?

   _____

   _____

   _____

★ ★

B. **True or False.** Circle true or false. Write the sentences from the story that explain your answer.

1. True or false? In 1851, Isaac Singer builds the first sewing machine.

   _____

   _____

2. True or false? When he is twelve years old, Singer runs away from home because he wants to be a mechanic.

   _____

   _____

3. True or false? During the "sewing machine wars" Isaac Singer cannot manufacture his machine.

   _____

   _____

4. True or false? Installment plan is an idea that influences how people buy things.

   _____

   _____

5. True or false? The sewing machine helps millions of women who can now stay home and sew.

   _____

   _____

6. True or false? After manufacturing sewing machines for a long time, Isaac Singer becomes very rich and moves to France.

   _____

   _____

Chapter Eight, Story Two

The Wright Brothers and Their Flying Machine

The dream of being able to fly is as old as human history. The stories of all nations tell of people who can fly. Sometimes, in these stories, they fly on magic carpets. Sometimes they tie wings to their bodies and fly away as easily as birds. But that only happens in dreams and stories.

In the early twentieth century, the age of industry and invention, scientists and engineers search for a way to make a flying machine that is heavier than air.

Two brothers, Orville and Wilbur Wright, are not scientists or engineers. Neither one even graduates from high school. They own a shop in Dayton, Ohio, where they repair bicycles. Flying is their greatest interest in life and they read almost everything that is written on the subject.

Wilbur and Orville build and learn to fly gliders, which are heavier-than-air planes without motors. They discover that much of what they read about flying is wrong. They begin to depend on their own experiments and observation. They notice that big birds balance in the air by turning the tips of their wings and they discover a way to make their glider wings turn, too.

The first biplane glider they build (biplane means that there are two wings, one above the other) measures about five feet from wing-tip to wing-tip. Gradually, their gliders get bigger. The brothers find some land in Kitty Hawk, North Carolina, where the wind is usually right for testing their planes, and where there is soft sand for rough landings. By 1901 they are testing gliders big enough to carry a person. Wilbur and Orville take turns. Whichever one is flying lies flat on the lower wing and moves his weight, much as a bicycle rider does, to balance the plane.

Gliders are fun, but they are not practical transportation[6]. The Wright brothers begin to think about using an automobile engine to power their planes. They find that it is too heavy, and they finally develop the engine that they need in their own shop.

On December 14, 1903, the Wright Flyer is ready. It is a biplane with wings measuring over forty feet and it has an engine that drives two propellers[7] in opposite directions. The brothers toss a coin[8] to decide who flies first. Wilbur wins and takes off in the Flyer — which falls into the sand three and a half seconds later.

It takes three days to fix the plane. On December 17, Orville is the first pilot[9]. He flies one hundred and twenty feet and the flight lasts twelve seconds — only twelve seconds, but enough to prove that after thousands of years of wishing, man can fly.

Altogether, the Wright brothers test their plane four times that morning. On the last flight, Wilbur remains up in the air for fifty-nine seconds and flies eight hundred and fifty-two feet!

Orville and Wilbur are proud of themselves. They send a telegram to their father asking him to inform the newspapers of their success.

The newspapers aren't interested. They are tired of all the people who claim they can fly and turn out not to be able to. The Wrights can't even make the United States Army interested in the possibilities of the airplane as a war machine. It takes a while. In 1905, the Wright brothers make a flight of twenty-four miles. Now the whole world is interested.

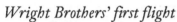

6   **transportation** — travel
7   **propellers** — blades that spin and propel, or move something forward
8   **toss a coin** — throw a coin in the air, to decide something by the way it falls
9   **pilot** — a person who steers a ship or airplane

Wright Brothers' first flight

Library of Congress

Chapter Eight, Story Two
The Wright Brothers and Their Flying Machine

Exercises

A. **Reading Comprehension — Discussion and Writing.** Choose two questions to discuss with a partner. Write the rest, looking back at the story, or using your own words.

1. How do Wilbur and Orville Wright learn about gliders and how do they fly?

_____

_____

_____

2. How do the brothers test their planes?

_____

_____

_____

3. What do they do when their plane finally flies eight hundred and fifty-two feet in the air?

_____

_____

_____

4. Why aren't the newspapers interested in the Wright brothers' flight?

_____

_____

_____

★ ★

B. **Vocabulary.** Fill in the blanks with the correct word.

1. Orville and Wilbur Wright are not ª·_____ or ᵇ·_____.

2. After they discover that many things they read are wrong, they begin to depend on their ᶜ·_____ and ᵈ·_____.

3. The Wright Flyer is a ᵉ·_____ which falls after three and a half seconds.

4. The newspapers are tired of so many people who ᶠ·_____ they can fly.

5. They even try to interest the United States Army in the plane as a
ᵍ·_____ ʰ·_____.

6. Their ⁱ·_____ of twenty-four miles makes everyone interested.

Chapter Nine, Overview

The Land of Opportunity

Between 1820 and 1920, over fifty million Europeans leave their own countries and go to live somewhere else. It is the greatest movement of population in history. Of these fifty million, thirty-five million choose to come to the United States of America.

Their reasons for coming are not so very different from those of the Pilgrims and the other colonists — immigrants too, every one of them. There is plenty of land, and it is cheap. There is a job for anybody who wants to work. In the land of opportunity, everybody has equal rights. The American constitution says so.

Until the middle of the nineteenth century, most of the immigrants are English or Swedish or German Protestants who fit into American life quickly and easily. But in 1846 a plant disease destroys all the potatoes in Ireland. A million Irish die of hunger and a million more leave their country forever. Many of them go to the United States.

Americans don't welcome the Roman Catholic Irish as warmly as they do the English or the Germans. The Irish have to take the jobs that nobody else wants. They build the roads, dig the coal, carry the bricks. They continue to do the hard work of the nation until another big immigration brings Poles, Russians, Polish and Russian Jews, Hungarians, Italians, Greeks, Portuguese, Rumanians, Bulgarians, Lithuanians, Ukrainians, and many, many others.

These people have the same hopes and dreams as those who arrive before them. They also want a better life. But the immigrants from southern and eastern Europe are even less welcome than the Irish. They don't speak English, their religion and their customs are different, their clothes are strange. Worse, they are willing to work hard for so little money that American workers fear immigrants are going to take away their jobs.

Bad feeling against immigrants grows. In 1924, congress makes a law to limit immigration. To do that, congress sets quotas, which are the numbers of people allowed to enter the United States from all other countries. These quotas allow in many more immigrants from Great Britain and Germany than they do from Russia or Italy. Very few Asians or Africans are permitted to come in.

Immigration from Mexico and Latin America is much harder to control because it's not too difficult to get across the border. The big farmers don't really want to control it because these are the people who do farm work. Especially after World War I begins, they need as many farm workers as they can get.

Though it is unjust, the 1924 Act of Congress to limit immigration remains the law of the United States for more than forty years. But slowly, American trade with Asian countries becomes very important. This helps change the immigration laws. In 1965, another act of congress removes the quota laws to admit great numbers of Asians: Japanese, Chinese, Filipinos, Koreans, Indians, Pakistanis, and Pacific Islanders, and a few years later, Vietnamese.

Chapter Nine, Overview
The Land of Opportunity

Exercises

A. **Reading Comprehension — Discussion and Writing.** Choose three questions to discuss with a partner. Write the rest, looking back at the story, or using your own words.

1. Why do thirty-five million people come to the United States between 1820 and 1920?

_____

_____

_____

2. Why do so many Irish immigrate in the middle of the nineteenth century?

_____

_____

_____

3. How do Americans feel about the great numbers of immigrants from all over the world?

_____

_____

_____

★ ★ ★ ★ ★ ★ ★ ★ ★ ★ ★ ★ ★ ★ ★ ★ ★ ★ ★

4. How does congress respond to bad feelings against the immigrants in 1924?

_____

_____

_____

5. What helps to change the quota laws?

_____

_____

_____

B. Choose the best answer for these sentences.

1. Millions of immigrants come to the United States in the middle of the nineteenth century because

   a. there are opportunities to work.
   b. there is plenty of cheap land.
   c. everyone has equal rights under the constitution.

2. Irish immigrants

   a. are willing to work at hard jobs.
   b. are welcome because they are willing to word at hard jobs for little pay.
   c. fit easily into American life.

3. Farm workers come to the United States from Mexico and Latin America because

   a. the quota laws allow them to immigrate.
   b. a plant disease in their country causes them to die of hunger.
   c. they are needed to work on American farms.

4. Quota laws

   a. are laws to limit immigration.
   b. allow anyone to enter the United States who wishes to come.
   c. make immigrants work hard for very little money.

Chapter Nine, Story One

The Statue[1] of Liberty

When a ship carrying immigrants arrives in New York Harbor, the first thing the passengers see is the Statue of Liberty. In 1886, when the statue is new, it is taller than any building in New York. From the bottom of the pedestal, the support on which the statue stands, to the tip of Liberty's torch[2], it is three hundred and five feet high.

Today, more than a hundred years later, the two hundred thousand pounds of copper metal which cover the statue are green from the salty ocean air. But in the beginning, the Statue of Liberty shines as brightly as a new penny in the sun.

Most immigrants make the long voyage to the United States in the dark bottom of a ship where passengers without much money are crowded together. When they finally arrive and come up into the light and the fresh air, they see the Statue of Liberty waiting for them, holding her torch up high. For most, it is an experience they never forget. Liberty is hope, she is courage, she is the promise of America.

The statue is a gift from the people of France to the people of the United States to celebrate one hundred years of American independence. The famous French sculptor[3], Frederic Bartholdi, has the idea of building something big and important for this special occasion. The great engineer, Alexandre Eiffel, builder of the Eiffel Tower in Paris, makes the strong steel structure which supports the statue. The whole project is so difficult and ambitious that it cannot possibly be ready in time for July 4, 1876, but the statue's great right arm, which is forty-two feet long, does arrive later that year.

France is paying for the statue, but expects the United States to pay for the pedestal on which the statue stands. At first the American people don't want to give money for this cause. Most newspapers are unfriendly to the project and wealthy people are not interested. But Joseph Pulitzer, who owns a newspaper and is an immigrant himself, finds a way to help.

He promises to print in his newspaper the name of any man, woman or child who sends in money to help pay for Liberty's pedestal. The money comes in, a dollar or two at a time, until finally there is enough.

On October 28, 1886, a million people waving American flags march down Fifth Avenue in New York to welcome the Statue of Liberty. Even now, in our time, Miss Liberty has two million visitors every year. When they enter the pedestal, they read the famous poem by Emma Lazarus that hangs on the wall. In her poem, the poet imagines that the statue is speaking to the countries of the Old World. "Give me your tired, your poor…" Liberty says. The daughter of immigrant parents, Emma Lazarus

The Statue of Liberty. Scene from an immigrant ship entering New York harbor

understands very well what it means to be tired and poor and come at last to the land of opportunity.

Today, most visitors ride to the top of the Statue of Liberty in an elevator, but some still prefer to climb the 154 steps that lead into the statue's crown[4]. There they can stand and look down at the ships in the water. Perhaps some of them remember the nineteenth century immigrant boats and the passengers arriving from so many different countries with their children, their suitcases, and their dreams of a better life.

[1] **statue** — a figure made by an artist, usually of wood, metal or clay
[2] **torch** — light
[3] **sculptor** — an artist who makes figures
[4] **crown** — anything worn on the head that decorates, and gives importance: usually worn by kings

★ ★ ★ ★ ★ ★ ★ ★ ★ ★ ★ ★ ★ ★ ★ ★ ★ ★ ★ ★

Chapter Nine, Story One
The Statue of Liberty

Exercises

A. **Reading Comprehension — Discussion and Writing.** Choose three questions to discuss with a partner. Write the rest, looking back at the story, or using your own words.

1. Describe the Statue of Liberty.

_____

_____

_____

2. Why does France want to give the Statue of Liberty to the United States on July 4, 1876?

_____

_____

_____

3. Who is Joseph Pulitzer, and how does he help raise money for Liberty's pedestal?

_____

_____

_____

4. In Emma Lazarus' poem, to whom is Liberty speaking, and what does she ask?

_____

_____

_____

5. What does the Statue of Liberty mean to arriving immigrants when they see her?

_____

_____

_____

B. **Complete the Sentences.** Draw a line between the words on the left and the words on the right to make a correct sentence.

1. The tip of Liberty's torch is   a. opportunity in America.

2. The Statue of Liberty is hope, and courage, and the promise of   b. send in money to pay for the pedestal.

3. Men, women and children   c. a shiny penny.

4. Joseph Pulitzer is an immigrant who   d. three hundred and five feet from the bottom.

5. Copper is the color of   e. owns a newspaper.

Chapter Nine, Story Two

The Chinese in California

Just as immigrants from Europe cross the Atlantic Ocean and arrive in New York, immigrants from China cross the Pacific Ocean and arrive in San Francisco.

These are hard times in China. To make a living for their families, many men must leave their country and try to get work somewhere else. Most of them intend to return home some day, maybe with enough money to buy a little piece of land.

In 1849, news of the discovery of gold in California reaches China. Twenty thousand Chinese sail away to America, hoping to find good fortune there. Few do. The miners already working in the gold fields don't want to share the gold with these strange-looking men. Their skin is a different color, they speak a language nobody can understand, and they wear their hair in a braid which Americans call a pig-tail. Like the Irish immigrants, the Chinese have to accept the jobs other people don't want: working in restaurants and washing clothes.

Still, the Chinese continue to come. At this time, two great railroads are being built which are some day going to connect, making it possible to cross the United States by train. The managers of the Central Pacific Railroad, which is laying track[5] from the West toward the East, don't at first plan to hire any Chinese. But the work is so dangerous and difficult that white workers often just pick up their pay checks and don't come back. In the end, of the ten thousand workers who build Central Pacific, nine thousand are Chinese. When the railroad tracks reach the great mountains called the High Sierras, and it becomes necessary to cut through solid rock, the Chinese workers are lowered in baskets to drill holes for explosives, like gunpowder. Sometimes these explode too soon, and the workers are killed. Sometimes the ropes that pull the baskets up break and the men fall to their death thousands of feet below.

The Chinese are paid $26 a month for doing this work. When they learn that white workers get $35 a month for doing less, they go on strike, but their strike is soon broken.

Employers like to hire Chinese immigrants because they work so hard for so little. They are very unpopular with most of the white workers for exactly the same reason.

In 1873, there is a depression[6] in the United States. Mines and factories close. Jobs are hard to get. American workers are afraid that the Chinese, because they work for low wages, will take away their jobs. There are meetings and marches asking the government to stop Chinese immigration. In California, laws are passed to keep Chinese out of schools and hospitals and to prevent employers from hiring them. Violent acts against Chinese are common. People think it is fun to attack a "China-

Railroad construction, ca. 1900

man" and cut off his pigtail.

In 1882, congress passes an Exclusion[7] Law which stops the immigration of Chinese workers and prevents any Chinese from becoming citizens of the United States.

Other acts of congress prevent Chinese women, even the wives of Chinese now living in America, from entering this country. Most Chinese don't have enough money to pay for a boat ticket to go back home. Many of these immigrants never see their families again. By 1890, there are twenty-seven Chinese men for every one Chinese woman in the United States. Most of these men, prevented by law and by custom from marrying white women, live lonely lives in one or another American Chinatown.

Years later, in 1943, the United States and China are both fighting on the same side in the war against Japan. Congress makes new laws which allow Chinese people to become American citizens.

[5] **track** — metal rails that wheels of railroad cars ride on
[6] **depression** — a time of unemployment and falling prices and wages
[7] **exclusion** — the keeping out, or refusal to admit someone or something

★ ★ ★ ★ ★ ★ ★ ★ ★ ★ ★ ★ ★ ★ ★ ★ ★ ★ ★

Chapter Nine, Story Two
The Chinese in California

Exercises

A. **Reading Comprehension — Discussion and Writing.** Choose three questions to discuss with a partner. Write the rest, looking back at the story, or using your own words.

1. How do the Chinese get to America?

_____

_____

_____

2. Why do they leave China?

_____

_____

_____

3. What kinds of jobs do they find in America?

_____

_____

_____

4. Why does congress pass the Exclusion Law?

_____

_____

_____

5. After many years, why does congress change the old laws?

_____

_____

_____

B.   Fill in the correct words from the story to complete these sentences.

1. The miners who are already in the gold fields _____.

2. When the Chinese workers learn the white workers get $35.00 a month for doing less, _____.

3. Of the ten thousand workers who build the Central Pacific, _____
_____.

4. By 1890, there are twenty-seven Chinese men _____.

Chapter Ten, Overview

Over There (Part One)

In the summer of 1914, Americans are more interested in the Ford Model T automobile, now selling for under $500.00, than they are in the murder of an unknown Austrian duke. The Archduke Franz Ferdinand and his wife are shot down by a young Serb. Most Americans don't even know where Serbia is. They don't know or care that in Serbia the people are fighting for their freedom. Austria-Hungary declares war against Serbia, but that doesn't have anything to do with America, does it?

Unfortunately, it does. All the countries of Europe have open or secret agreements with other countries. France, Russia, Great Britain, and Serbia have agreements with each other. They are called the Allies. Germany, Austria-Hungary, Bulgaria and Turkey have agreements with each other. They are the Central Powers. The murder of the Archduke Franz Ferdinand is the match that sets Europe on fire and starts World War I. Austria-Hungary wants to punish Serbia for killing the Austrian archduke. Russia has an agreement to defend Serbia. One by one the countries of Europe choose sides. The war becomes a big war, a war for trade, for land, for influence, for colonies and for world power. Ten million soldiers lose their lives in this war, and twenty million others die of hunger and disease. It is at this date the worst war in human history, a war in which new weapons[1], poison gas, airplanes and tanks are used for the first time.

At the beginning, some Americans are on the side of the English and others are on the side of the Germans, but most people still believe the war is none of America's business. Now German soldiers march into France. It seems to many people in America that Germany means to take over Europe. American businesses begin lending millions of dollars to England and France to help them buy war material. German submarines, called U-boats, hide under the ocean and attack United

UCLA

Model T Ford

States ships. Americans are angry.

On May 1, 1915, a U-boat sinks the British passenger ship, Lusitania. 1198 passengers are lost, including 128 Americans. As a result of this submarine action, the United States moves a little closer to war. In the same month, Italy comes into the war on the side of the Allies.

In France, the armies of the Allies and the Central Powers face each other from two long lines of trenches[2].

"Over the Top" — *trench warfare*

They are sometimes only a few hundred yards apart. For thirty-two months this trench war continues, with neither side winning or losing much. Both sides waste the lives of their soldiers in hopeless battles. The men are in the trenches for days at a time. They drink dirty water. They chew rotten bread. Meanwhile, the commanding officers on both sides live in the best French country houses and drink fine wine with their excellent dinners. The common soldier begins to wonder what he is fighting and dying for. In the French army, many soldiers refuse to obey their officers.

In Russia a revolution is going on. Some Russian soldiers are called back to protect the Czar, their king. They kill their officers and join the revolution.

In America, anger against Germany grows. For a while, U-boat activity slows down. Then it starts up again. President Woodrow Wilson now makes a decision. On April 2, 1917, he asks congress for a declaration of war, a war that he hopes will be the last one: a war to end all wars.

[1] **weapons** — arms, or instruments used in fighting
[2] **trenches** — long, narrow openings in the ground, from which the earth is thrown up in front for protection during battle

★ ★

Chapter Ten, Overview
Over There (Part One)

Exercises

A. **Reading Comprehension — Discussion and Writing.** Choose four questions to discuss with a partner. Write the rest, looking back at the story, or using your own words.

1. What are the countries of the Central Powers?

_____

_____

_____

2. What are the countries of the Allies?

_____

_____

_____

3. How does the killing of Archduke Franz Ferdinand start World War I?

_____

_____

_____

4. For what reasons do the countries of Europe go to war?

_____

_____

_____

5. What causes Americans to be angry with Germany?

_____

_____

_____

6. What are the new weapons of war?

_____

_____

_____

7. What does President Wilson do on April 2, 1917?

_____

_____

_____

B.   Choose the best ending to answer each question.

1. When war begins in Europe in 1914, America

   a. makes an agreement with the Allies.
   b. cares that Serbia is fighting for its freedom.
   c. is very interested in the Ford Model T automobile.

2. World War I

   a. sets Europe on fire.
   b. is a war for trade, land, influence, colonies and world power.
   c. causes the Allies and the Central Powers to make an agreement with each other in France.

3. While soldiers fight each other in France,

   a. neither side wins or loses much.
   b. soldiers of the French army waste their lives.
   c. the Allied forces begin winning the war.

Chapter Ten, Overview

Over There (Part Two)

The first American soldiers, called Yankees, or Yanks, arrive in Paris on the Fourth of July, 1917. Looking wonderful in their new uniforms, they parade from the Tomb of the Emperor Napoleon to the Tomb of Lafayette. "Lafayette, we are here!" says the Yankee officer in charge. He says it in French and Paris goes wild. All of France falls in love with the young Americans.

The Allied soldiers are sick of war, sick of death and suffering. They can't believe their eyes when the well-dressed, well-fed Yankees take up their position in the trenches cheerfully singing a song that is a big hit in America. The words "Over There" mean, "over there in France."

"Over There, Over There,
"The Yanks are coming, the Yanks are coming,
"And we won't go home till it's over, Over There."

The war is going badly for the Allies. The Russian Czar is overthrown by a revolution and the new government of Russia, now known as the Soviet Union, signs a peace treaty with Germany. The Germans are preparing to race to Paris and victory. The hard-fighting Americans bring new courage to the tired French and English soldiers. Together, they turn back the German attacks and save Paris. The Germans, so sure they are going to win, are losing the war.

On November 6, 1918, in a railroad car hidden in a French forest, the German representatives surrender and sign the Armistice agreement that puts an end to the fighting.

At eleven o'clock on November 11, 1918 — the eleventh hour of the eleventh day of the eleventh month — all the guns of Europe fall silent. It is Armistice Day, at last, the day that all the soldiers on both sides lay down their arms or guns. Of the Yankee forces, 126,000 remain buried Over There, never to come home again.

The whole world celebrates the Armistice. While everyone is dancing in the streets, and kissing and hugging, the seeds of World War II are already in the ground, waiting to grow.

Chapter Ten, Overview
Over There, Part Two

Exercises

A. **Reading Comprehension — Discussion and Writing.** Choose two questions to discuss with a partner. Write the rest, looking back at the story, or using your own words.

1. Why does the Yankee officer say to the people of France, "Lafayette, we are here!"

   _____

   _____

   _____

2. Why does the war begin to go better for the Allies in 1917?

   _____

   _____

   _____

3. What does the Armistice mean?

   _____

   _____

   _____

4. What is the price to America of ending the war?

   _____

   _____

   _____

B. Choose the best answer for each sentence.

1. The Allied soldiers

   a. are called Yanks, or Yankees.
   b. are well-dressed and well-fed.
   c. are sick of war, death and suffering.

2. The Soviet Union

   a. is the new government of Russia.
   b. is headed by the Russian Czar.
   c. signs a peace treaty with Germany.

3. When the Armistice agreement is signed,

   a. 126,000 Yankee soldiers come home.
   b. World War II starts.
   c. all the soldiers lay down their arms.

Chapter Ten, Story

The War to End All Wars (Part One)

In 1912, Woodrow Wilson, a Democrat, is elected president of the United States.

Almost immediately there is trouble in Latin America. President Wilson has good intentions. He wants to respect the independence of Central and South American countries. But U.S. Marines are already protecting American business in Nicaragua and Santo Domingo, and the U.S. is being pushed by American businessmen who own mines and railroads in Mexico to take sides in a Mexican Revolution. Wilson at first refuses, but the Mexican problem does not go away. Instead, it gets more complicated and more dangerous. The resident now feels that he must send in the Marines. They land in Veracruz, Mexico, and take that city at the cost of several hundred Mexican lives. It is a difficult time for Wilson. He avoids war with Mexico only with the help of the leaders of Chile, Brazil and Argentina who step in to calm the situation.

In 1914, the year that World War I begins in Europe, Woodrow Wilson's first wife dies. A year later he meets and marries Edith Galt who becomes his best and closest friend. Through the long, hard years of the war, she is always at his side, always ready and able to help.

At first, it is Wilson's intention to keep the United States out of the war, but that becomes difficult to do. U.S. manufacturers are getting rich by making, selling and shipping war material to the Allies. When U-boats sink their ships, they expect their government to do something about it.

Now the president is not so sure he can keep America out of the war. He's not at all sure that he should. The danger from U-boats to American ships increases each day. More important, he believes the United States simply can't let Germany, Austria-Hungary and Turkey win the war. The threat to democratic Europe is now very real.

Wilson can no longer delay his decision as president. He asks congress to declare war against Germany and the Central Powers. His face is white as he tells congress, "It is a fearful thing to lead this great, peaceful people into war." But, he says, "The world must be made safe for democracy."

While Woodrow Wilson is sending American soldiers to protect democracy in Europe, it is in some danger at home. Congress passes laws to punish anyone who speaks out against the war. It is a time when neighbors are suspicious of neighbors, when schools are not allowed to teach the German language, when musicians are afraid to play the great music of German composers like Beethoven. This is not what President Wilson wants for his country, but is one of the bad things that can happen when a nation goes to war.

Chapter Ten, Story
The War to End All Wars (Part One)

Exercises

A. **Reading Comprehension — Discussion and Writing.** Choose two questions to discuss with a partner. Write the rest looking back at the story, or using your own words.

1. Why are American marines in Nicaragua, Santo Domingo, and later in Mexico?

   _____

   _____

   _____

2. What reasons does Wilson have to ask congress to declare war against Germany and the Central Powers?

   _____

   _____

   _____

3. What happens to democracy at home in the United States?

   _____

   _____

   _____

Chapter Ten, Story

The War to End All Wars (Part Two)

The war becomes Woodrow Wilson's life. He feels that it is his personal responsibility to arrange the kind of peace treaty that will make another war impossible.

As the end of the war comes closer and it is certain that the Central Powers are going to lose, Wilson works night and day on his program for peace. This program has fourteen main points, or ideas. Wilson strongly believes that his Fourteen Points should become part of the peace treaty which Germany and the Allies are going to sign at Versailles, France. The Fourteen Points include freedom of the seas for all ships, and independence for Poland, Yugoslavia and Czechoslovakia. They also include a League of Nations, a kind of world congress, to which all countries send representatives, and where they can come to settle their differences peacefully.

On December 4, 1919, less than a month after Armistice Day, President Woodrow Wilson sails to France. His purpose is to persuade the leaders of France, England and Italy to accept his Fourteen Points. The people of Paris give Wilson a hero's welcome, but the leaders of the Allies are not so friendly. The premier of France tells the prime minister of Great Britain, "Mr. Wilson bores me with his Fourteen Points; why, God Almighty has only ten!"

Wilson fights like a tiger for his program, and he is able to save some of it. He is especially happy that the leaders of Europe agree with his idea for a League of Nations. But in return, the president has to accept a peace treaty with Germany that he doesn't like, that he fears may lead to war again. Already, secret agreements between Britain, France and Italy divide up large parts of defeated Germany. In addition to the land they want, the Allies demand that Germany pay very large amounts of money. Wilson hopes for "peace without victory, peace among equals." The other Allied leaders want punishment and revenge. Wilson is learning that it is easier to win a war than to make a peace. How long, he wonders, can Germany accept this Treaty of Versailles?

Back in the United States, Wilson, a Democrat, discovers that the Republican congress does not intend to support either the peace treaty or the League of Nations. Wilson decides to take the issue directly to the people. On September 3, 1919, the president begins a three-week train trip all through the Middle West and Far West. He stops at twenty-nine towns and cities along the way. America must support the

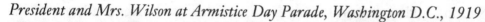

Versailles Treaty and the League of Nations, he tells the citizens. Already tired from his trip to Europe, President Wilson, whose health is never good, suffers a stroke[1]. Unable to stand, walk or talk, he is rushed back to the White House. He gets a little better in time, but is never well again. For many months, President Wilson is not seen by any official, any congressman, any newspaper reporter. People wonder who is acting as president. Can it be Mrs. Wilson?

The most important work of Wilson's life goes down to defeat. The United States does not join the League of Nations. Without support from the powerful United States, the League is not able to keep the peace. The world again begins to move slowly but surely toward war. Deaf, almost blind, looking years older than his age, Woodrow Wilson dies on February 3, 1924.

[1] **stroke** — a sudden attack of paralysis, as when a person is not able to move certain parts of the body.

President and Mrs. Wilson at Armistice Day Parade, Washington D.C., 1919

UCLA

Chapter Ten, Overview
The War to End All Wars (Part Two)

Exercises

A. **Reading Comprehension — Discussion and Writing.** Choose three questions to discuss with a partner. Write the rest, looking back at the story, or using your own words.

1. What is the Fourteen Points Program of Woodrow Wilson?

   _____

   _____

   _____

2. How much of Wilson's program do the European leaders accept?

   _____

   _____

   _____

3. How does the Republican congress feel about Wilson's plans?

   _____

   _____

   _____

4. What does Wilson do to gain support from the American people?

   _____

   _____

   _____

5. What happens to the League of Nations after Wilson becomes sick?

_____

_____

_____

B. **True or False.** Find a sentence in the story to support your answer.

1. True or false? The League of Nations is part of Wilson's Fourteen Point Program.

_____

_____

2. True or false? President Wilson is especially happy that Germany is going to pay large amounts of money.

_____

_____

3. True or false? Wilson discovers that congress is going to support the peace treaty and the League of Nations.

_____

_____

4. True or false? Wilson talks directly to the people about his plan.

_____

_____

5. True or false? To keep the peace, the League of Nations needs both Europe and the United States to support it.

_____

_____

Chapter Eleven, Overview

The Great Depression

For seven or eight years after the Armistice the American economy[1] is good and getting better every day. In 1928, Republican Herbert Hoover is elected the thirtieth president of the United States.

Newspapers and magazines of that period make their readers believe that everybody is busy spending and buying. Everybody is buying Ford's new automobile, radios, land in Florida, shorter and shorter skirts. Everybody hopes to get rich fast by buying stocks in the stock market. Stocks are parts or shares of America's business. Everybody knows that there is only one way for the value of stocks to go: up, up, up!

Today we know that not everybody is spending, not everybody is buying stocks in the stock market. The sad truth is that most Americans, six out of ten families in 1927 and 1928, are poor. On the farms, conditions are even worse than in the cities. Farmers are not able to pay back to the banks the money that they owe. Banks take farms away from farmers because they can't pay. The banks find they now own property nobody has money to buy. All over the country, banks begin to close. People with money in those banks lose it all. Bad times are coming. The whole world, not just the United States, is in a serious economic depression.

October 24, 1929, lives in history as Black Thursday. On that day, the stock market crashes. The price of stocks keeps falling, Everybody who owns stock wants to sell it and nobody wants to buy. Wall Street, the financial[2] center of New York, is crowded with people who now have no money and have no hope for the future.

So begin the gray, bitter years of the Great Depression. No one who lives

The great financial panic at New York Stock Exchange

Library of Congress

A Hooverville community, 1936

through those years ever forgets what it feels like not to have a job, or a home, or food for the children. Engineers, lawyers, businessmen sell apples on street corners to earn a little money because there is no other work for them to do. In some cities, eighty percent of the working people have no jobs.

To people who are hungry, who have no place to sleep safe from rain and snow, President Hoover begins to seem like a cold, heartless man. They believe that he is willing to help banks and businesses, but he doesn't want the government to vote money for unemployed people. People make up new words: "Hoovervilles" are little settlements where homeless people live in empty boxes or in tiny houses made from old bed springs, old pieces of wood, and other thrown away things. "Hoover blankets" are newspapers with which people cover themselves at night to try to keep out the freezing wind.

In 1932, about 15,000 men, once U.S. soldiers in World War I, come to Washington D.C. They come to ask for early payment of the Soldiers' Bonus, extra money the government owes them. They build Hoovervilles near the Potomac River and wait for their government to act. The senate refuses to vote for the bonus. Very disappointed, some of the Bonus Marchers, as they call themselves, go home. Others stay, hoping they can influence the senate to change its mind. The president orders the army to chase them away. The Bonus Marchers try to fight back, but the army's swords, horses and tear gas are too much for them.

Many Americans, listening to the news on the radio, are angry that old soldiers are treated this way. Just wait until November, they tell each other. An election is coming. The Governor of New York, Franklin Delano Roosevelt, a Democrat, is running against President Herbert Hoover. The Republicans are promising, "two cars in every garage and a chicken in every pot." Roosevelt is promising, "a new deal for the American people."

1   **economy** — the management of a country's wealth
2   **financial** — regarding money matters

Chapter Eleven, Overview
The Great Depression

Exercises

A. **Reading Comprehension — Discussion and Writing.** Choose three questions to discuss with a partner. Write the rest, looking back at the story, or using your own words.

1. How do Americans feel about the economy after the Armistice of 1919?

_____

_____

_____

2. How do many farmers lose their farms in 1927 and 1928?

_____

_____

_____

3. What happens on October 24, 1929?

_____

_____

_____

4. How do people live, without money and jobs?

_____

_____

_____

5. Why do World War I soldiers march to Washington D.C.?

_____

_____

_____

6. How do many people begin to feel about the government of Herbert Hoover by November 1932?

_____

_____

_____

B. Choose the correct ending for each sentence.

1. Newspapers, before 1928, tell the American public that

   a. everyone is buying chickens.
   b. people are buying automobiles, land and stocks.
   c. farmers are getting poor.

2. The economic depression

   a. helps farmers pay back to the bank the money they owe.
   b. disappoints the Bonus Marchers.
   c. affects the whole world.

3. Bonus Marchers

   a. ask for "two cars in every garage and a chicken in every pot."
   b. ask for extra money from the government.
   c. elect Franklin D. Roosevelt in November.

Chapter Eleven, Story One

The Dust Bowl

The Great Depression of the 1930's comes as no surprise to American farmers. They are already suffering from hard times. Farm prices are falling and failing banks cannot lend farmers any more money. But when it seems that the farmer's problems can't possibly get any worse, they do.

In the spring and summer of 1930, almost no rain falls in the Central United States. It doesn't rain in 1934, or 1936, or 1937. The summers are fiery hot and the cruel sun cracks the dry earth in Texas, Oklahoma, Nebraska, Kansas, North and South Dakota. The sun bakes the earth and turns it to fine dust. Then the winds come and blow the dust away. Whole farms blow away in great black clouds of dust that hide the sun and turn morning into midnight. The places where this happens are known as the Dust Bowl.

Dust Bowl

UCLA

Many people prefer to blame the Dust Bowl on nature, on natural causes, such as too many years without rain. But bad use of the land is also a cause. In good years, with plenty of rain, farmers plow[3] up the grasslands to plant crops. Then, with the terrible dry years of the 1930's, the roots of dying crops can't hold the soil down.

Between 1930 and 1935, three and a half million people leave the Dust Bowl and go on the road, looking for some place else to live. They travel in old cars that break down every few miles, with everything they own tied on top. Or they walk, pushing wagons with their few possessions and their smallest children. About 300,000 come all the way to California. In California, everybody calls the newcomers "Okies," meaning that they come from Oklahoma, even if they are really from Texas or Kansas; it no longer matters.

The desire to come to California is easy to understand. The "Okies" remind each other that it is always warm there. Oranges grow everywhere, and there are plenty of jobs for anybody who wants to pick fruit.

The truth is that California fruit growers need only about 175,000 workers for the picking season. There are many more willing workers than there are jobs so the growers can hire good people to work for almost nothing. That is what happens. In the 1930's, whole families of California farm workers can't earn enough money to feed themselves. The problems of earning a living in California are different from the problems of farming in the Dust Bowl, but sometimes they seem just as hard.

[3] **plow** — dig up and turn over the earth

Chapter Eleven, Story One
The Dust Bowl

Exercises

A. **Reading Comprehension — Discussion and Writing.** Choose two questions to discuss with a partner. Write the rest, looking back at the story, or using your own words.

1. How do the dry years of the 1930's affect the farmers?

_____

_____

_____

2. What kind of lands do farmers plow up in order to plant crops, and what happens when they do?

_____

_____

_____

3. Why do so many farmers from the Dust Bowl go to California?

_____

_____

_____

4. What are the problems that the "Okies" find when they arrive in California?

_____

_____

_____

B. **Vocabulary.** Fill in the correct word using the list below.

use   blows   growers   fail   possessions

fiery   fall   season   crops

1. The land _____ away when the winds come, and the sun is _____ hot.

2. During the picking _____ there are too many workers for the jobs.

3. Farm prices _____, and banks _____.

4. There are too many workers for the number of jobs, so _____ pay the "Okies" almost nothing.

5. Roots of the dying _____ can't hold down the soil.

6. Good _____ of the land is important to growing crops, and to nature.

7. Many farmers take their families and all their _____ and move to California.

Chapter Eleven, Story Two

F.D.R.

Franklin Delano Roosevelt is born into a wealthy family and grows up the way children of the very rich do. The Roosevelt home at Hyde Park, New York, is large and beautiful, with servants, gardeners, dogs and horses — everything that helps to make life happy and comfortable.

Franklin goes to private schools where he is an average student. He is so attractive and so well-liked that he sees no reason to take life seriously. The only really serious thing he does as a young man, and he does it over his mother's objection, is to marry his cousin, Eleanor Roosevelt. Eleanor is neither pretty nor rich, but she has, as Franklin tells his angry mother, a very good mind[4]. Theodore Roosevelt, who is Eleanor's uncle and Franklin's cousin, is now the president of the United States. He comes to the wedding and steals all the attention away from the young couple.

To everyone's surprise — is he following the example of cousin Theodore? — Franklin Roosevelt decides to go into politics. He gets himself elected a New York State Senator, and after that serves as President Woodrow Wilson's Assistant Secretary of the Navy. In 1920, the Democratic Party chooses Roosevelt, with his enthusiasm, his bright smile and his confident voice, to be its candidate for vice president. The Democrats lose the election, but Roosevelt is a great personal success and suddenly becomes a young man with a big political future.

That big future begins to look very small in 1921 when Roosevelt becomes ill with polio, at that time a disease which can't be prevented. He does not die, but his legs become paralyzed, useless, and he never walks again without help. His mother advises him to return to Hyde Park where he can live the quiet life of a rich man. Eleanor Roosevelt does not agree. It's only Franklin's legs that don't work, not his brain. She wants him to continue in politics.

In 1924, F.D.R. goes to the Democratic National Convention. He is there to name Al Smith as the candidate for president of the United States. Slowly, painfully, with so many eyes watching him, he pulls himself and his useless legs to the stage[5] of the convention. For this act of courage, the thousands of Democrats there applaud him for one hour and thirteen minutes.

Al Smith loses the election. He is Catholic and the United States is not ready to vote for a Catholic president.

But important Democrats do not forget Roosevelt. Eight years later, the United States is deep in the worst depression in history, but President Herbert Hoover is trying to tell the country that the depression is over. The Democratic Party chooses F.D.R., now governor of the state of New York, to run against Hoover in the 1932 election.

Gone is the young man who doesn't take life seriously. Now that he needs help himself, he is able to understand the poor, the hungry and the helpless. In person and on radio, he sounds like a man who cares, a man who promises a "new deal for the American people."

By a vote of 22,809,638 to 15,758,901, the greatest vote of confidence[6] in American history, Roosevelt is elected president and the age of the New Deal begins.

In the first hundred days, F.D.R. and his team of New Dealers act with speed and energy to fight the Great Depression. "The only thing we have to fear is fear itself," Roosevelt tells the country.

He immediately closes the banks to prevent more bank failures. Then he persuades congress to pass one law after another to give relief. His program gives jobs to jobless people. It encourages the growth of labor unions. It brings cheap electricity to parts of the country where it is needed. It insures loans so people will not lose their homes. It establishes a system of social security for older people. In those darkest days of the Depression, Mrs. Roosevelt travels all over the country, learning, helping, speaking out for justice, for women and minorities[7].

UCLA

Franklin Delano Roosevelt and Eleanor Roosevelt

In 1936, the year of the next presidential election, the American people send a very clear message. Roosevelt wins in every state except Maine and Vermont. While the Great Depression is not yet over, the United States is beginning to believe in itself again.

Americans are so busy fixing their economy that they don't pay enough attention to what is happening across the ocean. In Europe and in Asia, the political situation is growing darker and more threatening from day to day....

[4] **mind** — intelligence

[5] **stage** — a platform, or place to stand before an audience

[6] **vote of confidence** — vote of support

[7] **minorities** — refers to groups that are smaller and different by race, religion, or politics, than the larger controlling group

★ ★

Chapter Eleven, Story Two
F.D.R.

Exercises

A. **Reading Comprehension — Discussion and Writing.** Choose three questions to discuss with a partner. Write the rest, looking back at the story, or using your own words.

1. What kind of a young man is Franklin Delano Roosevelt?

   _____

   _____

   _____

2. What political jobs does F.D.R. have when he first goes into politics?

   _____

   _____

   _____

3. What happens to change F.D.R.'s life in 1921?

   _____

   _____

   _____

4. How does he show his courage at the Democratic National Convention?

   _____

   _____

   _____

5. What does Roosevelt do to fight the Depression?

_____

_____

_____

6. What does Mrs. Roosevelt do to help the American people?

_____

_____

_____

B. Choose the correct ending to these sentences.

1. F.D.R.

    a. suffers when he is very young, so he understands helpless people.
    b. is the uncle of President Theodore Roosevelt.
    c. marries his cousin, Eleanor, who has a very good mind.

2. After Roosevelt becomes ill with polio,

    a. he cannot ever walk again.
    b. his brain does not work.
    c. he cannot pull himself on to the stage at the Democratic National Convention.

3. Roosevelt names a Catholic, Al Smith, to run for president of the United States,

    a. but his mother advises him not to.
    b. and important Democrats applaud him for this.
    c. but Smith loses because the United States is not ready to vote for a Catholic president.

4. To try to end the Depression, Roosevelt

    a. goes into politics.
    b. with the help of congress, gets relief programs started.
    c. travels all over the country, speaking out for justice, women and minorities.

Chapter Twelve, Overview

World War II (Part One)

The Great Depression is especially bad in Germany. The Versailles Treaty, signed at the end of World War I, requires Germany to pay thirty-three billion dollars to Great Britain, France and the United States. This is more money than Germany can possibly pay. Inflation, which means the value of money goes down, and prices go up, is so serious that German money is worth almost nothing. When people go to the store, they have to carry their money in large bags.

Many Germans are angry. Former soldiers, who remember fighting for their country in the trenches of World War I, now can't get jobs, can't buy bread for their children. Everyone is looking for someone to blame. A new leader appears. He is Adolf Hitler, a powerful speaker who persuades most of the German nation to blame their troubles on the English, the French and especially the Jews. Hitler tells the German people that they belong to a superior race[1]. He wants Germany to be master of Europe. It is difficult to understand how such a man can become the head of the German government, but that is what happens. On January 30, 1933, Hitler's National Socialist Party, called Nazis, wins a national election.

During the same period, the Fascist Party of Benito Mussolini is already in power in Italy. Like Hitler, Mussolini governs through fear, violence and murder. In Japan, power is in the hands of generals who are already directing the invasion[2] of China. They secretly plan to take control of the whole Far East.

In the United States, most people don't understand what is happening across the oceans. Maybe they don't want to understand. If Europe wants another war, it isn't America's business. Everybody still remembers World War I as the "war to end all wars." They don't intend to send American boys to die in another European war. And they pay no attention to what is happening in the Orient.

The Versailles Treaty limits the German army to one hundred thousand men, but with nothing to stop him, Hitler builds the biggest army in history. This army is soon marching to war. On March 15, 1939, Germany invades Czechoslovakia, and still France and England do nothing. Afraid of another World War, they meet with Germany. They agree that Germany can keep part of Czechoslovakia in exchange for a promise of "peace in our time."

Hitler's army is at Germany's eastern border, facing the Soviet Union. Stalin, the Soviet leader, signs a separate treaty with Hitler to protect his country from Germany. This comes as a great shock to England and France. Now Hitler is free to move his army away from the Russian border and to launch an invasion of Poland.

145

While this is happening, Hitler is carrying out his plan to get rid of the Jews. He sends them to forced labor camps and prisons called concentration camps. Some of these have gas chambers, big rooms where many people can be killed at one time, by breathing in poison gas. Before the end of the war, six million Jews are murdered in these camps. Millions of others also die there: Catholics, Protestants, anyone who has the courage to speak against the Nazis.

In the early hours of September 1, 1939, German planes climb into the Polish skies and bomb the frightened people running out of their houses. In a few days it is all over. German tanks roll into Warsaw, the Polish capital. Germany and Russia divide up Poland.

On September 3, 1939, France and England finally declare war against Germany.

In the next few months, Hitler invades Denmark, Norway, Holland, Belgium and the rest of Czechoslovakia, and finally France. Now he is free to plan the invasion of Great Britain.

[1]   **race** — any of the different varieties of man
[2]   **invasion** — great number of people going into a place (to defeat it)

World War II, Europe

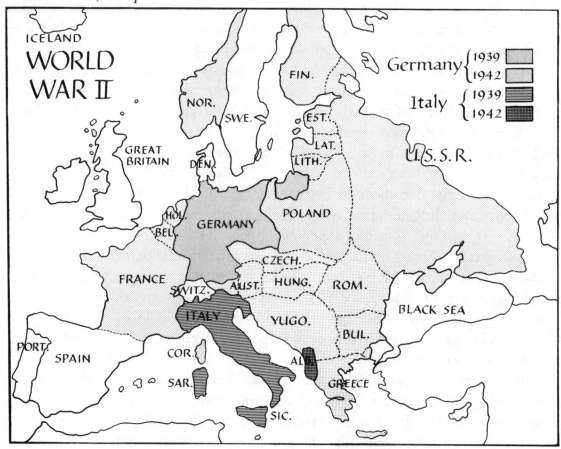

Chapter Twelve, Overview
World War II (Part One)

Exercises

A.   **Reading Comprehension — Discussion and Writing.** Choose three questions to discuss with a partner. Write the rest, looking back at the story, or using your own words.

1.   How do the Treaty of Versailles and the depression affect the lives of German people?

_____

_____

_____

2.   Why do the Germans elect Hitler?

_____

_____

_____

3.   Why don't France and England do anything when the German army invades Czechoslovakia?

_____

_____

_____

4.   Why does Stalin sign a treaty with Germany?

_____

_____

_____

5. What countries does Germany invade?

_____

_____

_____

B. **Vocabulary.** Fill in the correct words from the story.

1. Hitler is a powerful speaker who _____ the German people to

_____ their troubles on the English, French and the Jews.

2. Americans don't want to send their boys to fight another war in

_____. They remember the reason for World War I: to make the

world safe for _____.

3. To keep the Soviet Union safe from Hitler, Stalin signs a separate _____

_____ with Hitler.

C. **Definitions.** Find these words in your dictionary. Write their meaning, use each one in a sentence.

1. blame _____

_____

2. inflation _____

_____

3. persuade _____

_____

4. superior _____

_____

Chapter Twelve, Overview

World War II (Part Two)

Winston Churchill, the prime minister or head of the British government, knows that Hitler is going to attack England soon. He goes on the radio to tell the world, "We shall fight on the beaches; we shall fight in the hills; we shall never surrender."

Meanwhile, Franklin D. Roosevelt, just elected president for the third time, promises the American people that, "…this country is not going to war."

In his heart, though, he is not so sure. Roosevelt understands the danger to America if Hitler continues to take over Europe. He knows that he must do his best to prevent a German victory in Europe or Japanese control of the Pacific. He persuades congress to build a strong army and navy. He does not allow American business to sell iron or oil or war materials to Japan until it agrees to end the invasion of China. Premier Tojo, the leader of Japan, says he is willing to discuss the Chinese problem with the American government.

In 1941, two events happen that change world history.

On June 22, Hitler orders the invasion of the Soviet Union. Stalin, who still believes that his country is safe because of his treaty with Hitler, is not ready. The Red Army, as the Soviet forces are called, fights back hard, but the Germans keep winning. By December 2, German forces are just a few miles from Moscow, the capital of the Soviet Union.

On December 6, the Red Army begins a surprise attack that throws the Germans back many miles. With the help of the Russian winter and temperatures that are sometimes forty degrees below zero, the Red Army pushes the Germans away from Moscow, Stalingrad, Leningrad, and the other great Soviet cities Hitler wants to take. There is terrible loss of life on both sides. Moscow radio says, "Every seven seconds, a German soldier dies in Russia."

On December 7, while Premier Tojo's representatives still pretend to discuss the problem of China with the American government, Japanese bombers are secretly flying toward Pearl Harbor, in Hawaii, the home of the United States Navy's Pacific forces. It is a peaceful Sunday morning. Eight American battleships are sitting quietly in the water and American planes are lined up, wing to wing, on the air field. The Japanese representatives are at this very moment on their way to speak with the American secretary of state. Nobody expects any trouble.

Yelling their cry of victory, "Tora! Tora! Tora!" (Tiger! Tiger! Tiger!) the Japanese drop their bombs over Pearl Harbor. They destroy seven of the eight battleships and half the planes. Two thousand American sailors go down to their death inside the battleships.

It is the worst military loss in American history, but it unites the American people as never before. Now they are willing to fight until they win. When President Roosevelt asks congress, on December 8, to declare war against Japan, every senator and representative except one votes yes. Germany and Italy, who have a treaty with Japan, immediately declare war against the United States. By this time, about thirty-five countries, half the world's population, are at war.

4   **surrender** — to give in (to the enemy)

Pearl Harbor, December 7, 1941

Chapter Twelve, Overview
World War II (Part Two)

Exercises

A. **Reading Comprehension — Discussion and Writing.** Choose three questions to discuss with a partner. Write the rest, looking back at the story, or using your own words.

1. What is the danger at this time to Britain?

_____

_____

_____

2. What are the dangers to America at this time?

_____

_____

_____

3. What is the danger to the Soviet Union at this time?

_____

_____

_____

4. Why is the Japanese attack on Pearl Harbor not expected?

_____

_____

_____

5. What do Germany and Italy do when America declares war against Japan?

_____

_____

_____

B. **Vocabulary.** Choose a word or words to complete these sentences.

1. Winston Churchill goes on the _____ and tells the world that England will never _____.

2. Roosevelt does not allow America to sell Japan _____ or _____ until it agrees to remove its forces from China.

3. Hitler breaks his treaty with Stalin when he orders an _____ of the Soviet Union with his German forces.

4. On December 6, 1941, the Red Army begins a _____ against the German army.

5. The Japanese bombing of Pearl Harbor is the worst _____ in American history.

C. **Definitions.** Draw a line between words or phrases that have similar meaning. Use your dictionary when necessary.

1. forces   a. stop

2. elect   b. rule

3. surrender   c. choose

4. prevent   d. give up

5. control   e. armies

Chapter Twelve, Story One

Victory in Europe

Hitler's aim is to invade Great Britain but he is not able to do it. German planes bomb England night after night. At the same time, British and American planes fly over Germany every night, bombing roads, factories, cities.

While this is happening in the west, the Red Army, in the east, is slowly pushing the invaders out of the Soviet Union. The Yanks and the British are moving toward Germany. They are fighting their way north through Italy, and east through France. The war begins to go badly for Hitler. The German people, used to victory, now begin to know defeat.

In the month of April, 1945, important events happen very fast, one after another.

April 11: As American forces race toward Berlin, the capital of Germany, they stop to free the prisoners of the Buchenwald concentration camp. The Yanks see thousands of dead bodies, and thousands of prisoners, looking like skeletons[5], who are close to death. For the first time, the world truly understands what the Nazis are doing in their concentration camps.

April 12: Franklin Delano Roosevelt, now president of the United States for a fourth term, complains that he has a terrible headache. Then he falls forward. He never wakes up. F.D.R. is dead, at 63. Everywhere, people with tears in their eyes say good-bye to this great leader.

April 26: At 3:32 in the afternoon, Soviet soldiers who are moving to attack Berlin from the east, and American soldiers, who are moving toward Berlin from the west, see each other on opposite sides of the Elbe River, about fifty miles south of Berlin. It is a day to remember. Russians and Americans cross the river to hug each other, slap each other on the back, and drink to victory.

April 28: Benito Mussolini, the Fascist ruler of Italy, tries to escape to Switzerland with his mistress. He is dressed in a German uniform and he hopes that no one will know who he really is. A group of Italians who have been fighting the Fascists for a long time catch them both and kill them.

April 30: Hitler, with Eva, his bride of one day, and his closest friends and supporters live in a secret hiding place fifty feet below the streets of Berlin. He knows that the end is near. The sound of Russian guns is loud even there. Hitler poisons his favorite dog, gives poison to Eva, then shoots himself. His friends pour gasoline over both bodies and set them on fire.

A few days later, on May 7, 1945, Germany surrenders.

[5] **skeleton** — the bones of the body

★ ★

Chapter Twelve, Story One
Victory in Europe

Exercises

A. **Reading Comprehension — Discussion and Writing.** Choose two questions to discuss with a partner. Write the rest, looking back at the story, or using your own words.

1. What are German, British and American planes doing at this time?

_____

_____

_____

2. What is the RedArmy doing at this time?

_____

_____

_____

3. What direction are the American and British armies going at this time?

_____

_____

_____

4. On the afternoon of April 26, 1945, where are the Soviet and American armies? What do they do?

_____

_____

_____

B. **Vocabulary.** Fill in the correct word from the story.

1. The Americans and British are moving _____ through Italy, and _____ through France.

2. American and Russian soldiers finally meet in Germany at the Elbe River, close to _____.

3. Very soon after, the war in Europe ends. Germany _____.

C. **Definitions.** Write a word or phase that has a similar meaning to the <u>underlined</u> word or phrase.

1. Hitler wishes to <u>go into</u> Great Britain. He wants to _____.

2. Germans now understand <u>that they are losing the war.</u> They now understand __

   _____.

3. Hitler spends his last days underground, in <u>a place no one knows.</u> It is his

   _____.

Chapter Twelve, Story Two

Victory in Japan

The war in Europe is over, but the war with Japan goes on and on. It seems certain that the Japanese are losing, but how long is it going to take, and how many Americans are going to die if the United States now tries to invade Japan?

At Roosevelt's death, in 1945, his vice president, Harry S. Truman, becomes the thirty-second president of the United States. Only then does Truman learn about the Manhattan Project[6]. This project is so secret that almost nobody in the whole government even suspects[7] that it exists.

It all begins in 1938 and 1939 when many famous scientists come to America to escape from Nazi Germany and Fascist Italy. A group of these scientists warns President Roosevelt that it is possible for Germany to invent an atom bomb. They expect such a bomb to be many times more powerful than any bomb known before. President Roosevelt authorizes them to work on an atom bomb for the United States. This secret effort is called the Manhattan Project.

The Germans do try to make the atom bomb but are unsuccessful. They surrender soon after Truman becomes president. By that time, the Manhattan Project scientists are ready to test their first bomb on the desert in New Mexico, far away from cities or people.

The explosion produces a great ball of fire, brighter that the light of many suns. Even the scientists are frightened by its awful power. It is so frightening that many scientists do not want to continue with the project. They argue against dropping the bomb on Japan. They suggest, instead, that representatives from Japan be invited to see an atom bomb test. Then they will understand what can happen to their country if they do not surrender. This suggestion is not accepted and the war with Japan continues.

On July 26, 1945, President Truman, together with Britain's Winston Churchill and high military advisors demand Japan's complete surrender. Japan refuses. It is the president's decision to save American lives by ending the war with Japan as quickly as possible. He orders the bomb dropped.

On August 6, 1945, a United States plane drops the world's first atom bomb directly over an important Japanese military center, the city of Hiroshima. It explodes in the air and forms a fireball as hot as the sun. The fireball sucks up millions of tons of dust and becomes a terrible mushroom-shaped cloud. In the first second, sixty thousand buildings disappear. No one knows how many people die immediately, probably eighty thousand. The ones who die quickly are lucky. Thousands walk around with their ears and noses melting, their skin burned black. Perhaps even worse, many

U.S.S.R.

MANCHUKUO

JAPAN

CHINA

Hiroshima

Tokyo

Nagasaki

Burma Road

BURMA

OKINAWA

LAOS

THAILAND

CAM.

Manila

VIETNAM

PHILIPINES

MALAYA

Singapore

NEW GUINEA

NETHERLANDS E. INDIES

Guadalcanal

SOLOMON IS.

Tarawa

GILBERT IS.

MARIANA IS.

Guam

WAKE I.

MARSHALL IS.

MIDWAY IS.

ALEUTIAN ISLANDS

PACIFIC

Pearl Harbor

HAWAIIAN IS.

OCEAN

Japan ☐ 1930

WORLD WAR II

Occupied by Japan ☐ 1942

AUSTRALIA

World War II, Pacific

people become ill and die slowly, year after unhappy year, from the effects of the bomb.

The Japanese still do not surrender. They still have five thousand planes and about a million men in their armed forces. On August 9, the United States drops a second, even more powerful bomb over the Japanese city of Nagasaki.

On August 14, the government of Japan surrenders. World War II is over. Fifty million people are dead.

6 **project** — any kind of work that takes great planning
7 **suspect** — to think that something is likely: suppose

★ ★ ★ ★ ★ ★ ★ ★ ★ ★ ★ ★ ★ ★ ★ ★ ★ ★ ★ ★

Chapter Twelve, Story Two
Victory in Japan

Exercises

A. **Reading Comprehension — Discussion and Writing.** Choose two questions to discuss with a partner. Write the rest, looking back at the story, or using your own words.

1. Why does President Roosevelt set up the Manhattan Project?

    _____

    _____

    _____

2. How do many scientists feel about the atom bomb when they see it tested?

    _____

    _____

    _____

3. What reasons does President Truman have for dropping the atom bomb?

    _____

    _____

    _____

B. **Vocabulary.** Fill in blanks with words from the story.

1. The scientists who see the atom bomb test think it so _____ that they don't want to _____ with the project.

2. Japan seems to be losing the war, but refuses to _____.

3. Many Japanese people do not die immediately, but suffer year after year from the _____ of the atom bomb.

C. **Definitions.** Look up these words in your dictionary, and write a sentence for each one.

1. explain _____

   _____

2. duty _____

   _____

3. suggest _____

   _____

4. advisor _____

   _____

Chapter Thirteen, Overview

The Cold War

The good feelings that exist between the United States and the Soviet Union in the exciting weeks before Germany surrenders do not last long. Old suspicions[1] return stronger than before. The Soviet Union believes in communism. In a communist society, most property, such as land, factories, railroads and mines, belongs to everybody. The United States believes in capitalism, and is the most successful of all capitalist countries. In a capitalist society, most property belongs to individual people. Russians worry that the U.S., with its great economic power and its atom bomb, wants to rule the world. Americans worry that the Soviet Union, already master of so much of Eastern Europe, will encourage communist revolution in Greece, Italy, China, and the African nations.

In 1946, Winston Churchill puts the situation into unforgettable words. He says that there is an Iron Curtain between the Soviet countries and the rest of Europe. He warns that the Soviet Union is threatening the peace of the world.

This is the beginning of the Cold War. It is a war without a declaration of war by Congress, without a shot being fired. It is a long, hard struggle between two different societies, two different ways of thinking.

The Cold War continues, in one way or the other, until 1991. In that year, East Germans who live under the control of the Soviet Union, together with West Germans who are now part of democratic Europe, break down the ugly Berlin Wall that divides them. They take the first steps toward becoming one nation again.

But, way back in 1949, nobody can even imagine such an event. That is the year when the Soviet Union, more and more suspicious of American intentions, learns to make an atom bomb of its own. From that moment on, the United States is no longer the only country able to destroy the world.

In the same year, a revolutionary communist government takes power in China, to the great disappointment of the United States. When, in 1950, North and South Korea go to war against each other, the Russian and Chinese governments aid the North, while the United States helps the South.

The Cold War influences the exploration of space. On October 5, 1957, a strange little sound from outer space attracts the immediate attention of the whole world. It sounds like the cheep-cheep-cheep of a baby chicken, and it's rather funny, but it does not amuse the United States. The sound comes from a 185 pound steel ball that is speeding around the earth once every ninety minutes. This very first artificial[2] satellite[3] has a Russian name, Sputnik. It is the work of Russian scientists who are proud and happy to beat the United States in their race into the space age.

Inside the U.S., suspicion and bad feelings grow. Some Americans believe that there are communists in the government who are giving secret information to the Russians.

Sputnik, and the other Soviet successes in space produce a very great feeling of competition[4]. Generals, congressmen, newspapermen look for somebody to blame. They decide it is the fault of American schools for not teaching as much mathematics or science as the Russians do.

In 1960, John Fitzgerald Kennedy, a Democrat, defeats Republican Richard M. Nixon and becomes President of the United States. He tells the American people of his program to send a man to the moon before the year 1970. Congress allows twenty billion dollars to fund[5] Project Apollo, as it is called.

Nine years pass before that happens. By that time, Kennedy is dead, murdered before the eyes of thousands of people.

[1] **suspicion** — belief that someone is guilty or bad; distrust
[2] **artificial** — made by human work or art; not natural
[3] **satellite** — an object that revolves around the earth or moon
[4] **competition** — contest, or struggle
[5] **fund** — provide money for

★ ★

Chapter Thirteen, Overview
The Cold War

Exercises

A. **Reading Comprehension — Discussion and Writing.** Choose two questions to discuss with a partner. Write the rest, looking back at the story, or using your own words.

1. In what general ways are capitalism and communism different?

_____

_____

_____

2. How do the governments of the Soviet Union and the United States fight the Cold War in Korea?

_____

_____

_____

3. How do American generals, congressmen and newspapermen feel when the Russians put the satellite, Sputnik, into space?

_____

_____

_____

4. What plan has President Kennedy for competing with the Soviet Union in space?

_____

_____

_____

B. **True or False?** Circle true or false. Find the answers in the story to support your answer.

1. True or false? The Soviet Union makes the atom bomb in order to compete with the United States.

   _____

   _____

   _____

2. True or false? Americans believe that poor education in U.S. schools lets the Russians beat them in the space program.

   _____

   _____

   _____

3. True or false? The American government doesn't want to spend money on Kennedy's space program.

   _____

   _____

   _____

Chapter Thirteen, Story One

John Fitzgerald Kennedy

Joseph P. Kennedy, the grandson of poor Irish immigrants, becomes a very rich man before he is even thirty-five. He puts a million dollars in the bank for each of his nine sons and daughters. Kennedy says he does this to make them independent.

Not only is Mr. Kennedy a wealthy man, he is also important in politics. He makes up his mind that his oldest son, also named Joseph, is someday going to be president of the United States.

President John F. Kennedy, Feb. 1, 1963

Both young Joseph and his brother John, born two years later, fight in World War II. Joseph is killed while flying a bomber over France. The father decides that John is now responsible for becoming the Kennedy who goes to live in the White House.

In 1946, John Kennedy runs for congress from the state of Massachusetts. All his sisters and brothers and their husbands and wives work hard for his election. ("And don't forget," say his enemies, "how much money his father spends to get him to congress!")

On election day, the young Democrat, John Kennedy, easily defeats the Republican candidate. Six years later, he is elected to the United States Senate.

Senator Kennedy's friends call him "Jack." He is young, intelligent, easy to like. He has a beautiful wife, Jacqueline, and two delightful children. People high up in the Democratic Party begin to notice him. In 1960, he becomes the Democratic candidate for president and, by very few votes, defeats Republican Richard M. Nixon. Kennedy, at forty-three, is the first Catholic ever to be elected president of the United States.

From the first day, Kennedy faces serious problems. In Cuba, only ninety miles from Florida, Fidel Castro heads a communist government. Cubans who are against Castro, led by American officers, try to bring down the Cuban government, but fail. The United States and the Soviet Union, which supports Castro, almost go to war over Cuba. Kennedy wins a war of nerves when the Russians promise not to supply Cuba with war materials if the United States promises not to invade Cuba. The world watches as the two superpowers back away from a possible atomic war.

Meanwhile, in the United States, black citizens continue to demand equal rights.

Dr. Martin Luther King Jr., the great black leader, organizes a march of two hundred thousand people to Washington D.C. This is in support of a civil rights bill that Kennedy wants congress to pass. It is a grand moment in the non-violent civil rights movement. Even so, very little real progress is made. But Kennedy does help to end segregation and discrimination in public places, in schools, in housing and government jobs.

The president is not able to finish this work...or any work...

On November 22, 1963, President and Mrs. Kennedy are riding in an open car in Dallas, Texas. They are waving to the cheerful crowd which smiles and waves back. Suddenly there are gun shots. The president falls face down in his wife's lap. John Kennedy, forty-six years old, is dead.

Americans, shocked and frightened, spend the next days in front of their television screens. They see Dallas police arrest a man, Lee Harvey Oswald, for the murder of Kennedy. A few days later, they see a mysterious man shoot and kill Oswald. Finally, they see the president's funeral.

There are hundreds of books which try to explain the terrible events of those days. Questions are still being asked, and there are few answers. Even today, we do not know the whole truth.

Chapter Thirteen, Story One
John Fitzgerald Kennedy

Exercises

A. **Reading Comprehension — Discussion and Writing.** Choose two questions to discuss with a partner. Write the rest, looking back at the story, or using your own words.

1. How do Joseph P. Kennedy's ambitions affect his family?

_____

_____

_____

2. What happens in Cuba that nearly makes an atomic war possible?

_____

_____

_____

3. How does Martin Luther King support the civil rights bill?

_____

_____

_____

4. How does John Kennedy die?

_____

_____

_____

★ ★ ★ ★ ★ ★ ★ ★ ★ ★ ★ ★ ★ ★ ★ ★ ★ ★ ★ ★

B. **True or False?** Circle true or false. Find information in the story to support your answer.

1. True or false? John Kennedy has the support of his family when he runs for congress.

   _____

   _____

   _____

2. True or false? The Soviet government gives war materials to Cuba.

   _____

   _____

   _____

3. True or false? Some Cubans who don't support Castro's government try to invade Cuba by themselves.

   _____

   _____

   _____

4. True or false? The civil rights march on Washington, with two hundred thousand people, is a peaceful demonstration.

   _____

   _____

   _____

Chapter Thirteen, Story Two

Apollo 11 Goes to the Moon

After Sputnik and the other Russian successes in space, the United States organizes the Apollo Project, a special space exploration program. The purpose of the program is to catch up with Soviet Union and to make President Kennedy's promise come true: to send an American to the moon by 1970. Such an ambitious program costs billions of dollars. Some people think this money can be better spent fighting disease and hunger right here on earth. But the human desire to travel in space is as old as history. And even more, scientists need to understand the universe, and new technology[1] is making that possible.

The moon is about 238,000 miles away from earth. It has no air, no water, no weather. The moon's sky is always black, day or night, and the temperature is hundreds of degrees above zero in the daytime, hundreds of degrees below at night. Is it possible for a visiting astronaut[2] to live and breathe on the moon, even for a few hours?

It takes years for scientists to develop a suit which can protect an astronaut on the moon. It takes years for other scientists to develop a rocket with enough power to launch a spaceship toward the moon. Meanwhile, the Russians send up several spaceships of their own. In 1965, Alexei Leonov, a Russian astronaut, becomes the first person to walk in space. A few months later, an American astronaut, Edward H. White, does it too.

Under the Apollo program, Apollo 7, 8, 9 and 10 are successfully tested. On July 16, 1969, after so many years of hard work, Apollo 11 is finally ready. The three astronauts who are going on this, the most exciting voyage of all time, are Neil Armstrong, the commander of the Apollo moonship, Edwin E. Aldrin, and Michael Collins. Very early on the morning of July 16, all three are already wearing their spacesuits and are inside the rocket. Crowds of Americans come to see the launching of Apollo 11. In every country of the world, anyone who can get near a television is watching too. Excitement grows, even in the usually calm control rooms, where the men and women who work on the Apollo project all call together, "Go, baby, go! Go, baby, go!"

NASA

Apollo/Saturn V

At 9:32 a.m. Apollo 11 goes. Spitting red fire and black smoke, the great rocket ship, taller than the Statue of Liberty, takes off at a speed of 6,000 miles an hour. After the rocket gets away from the pull of the earth, it travels much faster. Four days later, Armstrong and Aldrin leave the space ship and fly the rest of the way in a small machine specially made for the moon landing. They call the machine the Eagle. Collins remains in the Apollo and flies around the moon twenty-five times, waiting for the moment when the Eagle and the other two astronauts return to the spaceship for the flight back to earth...if everything goes well...if nothing unexpected happens...

Edwin Aldrin walks on the moon

The Eagle lands perfectly. Neil Armstrong, his heart beating very fast, walks down the ladder and makes the first human footprint on the moon. He says, "That's one small step for a man, and one giant leap[3] for mankind."

Aldrin comes out of the Eagle to join Armstrong. The two men take pictures, collect rocks and do scientific experiments. They also place an American flag on the moon, and it is certainly there to this day, for there is no wind or rain to wear it out.

Now the question is, can Armstrong and Aldrin return to the Apollo? They can. The Eagle takes off from the moon, meets and joins the Apollo in space. When all three astronauts are together again in the Apollo, they set the Eagle free to fly forever and ever around the moon.

Planet Earth, as seen from behind the moon

On July 24, at a speed of 24,000 miles an hour, Apollo 11 approaches the earth. At 12:22 p.m. the astronauts splash down into the Pacific Ocean. The great adventure is over and the three men are home, safely home on planet earth.

1 **technology** — the study of practical arts and sciences
2 **astronaut** — a person trained in space flight
3 **leap** — jump

★ ★

Chapter Thirteen, Story Two
Apollo 11 Goes to the Moon

Exercises

A. **Reading Comprehension — Discussion and Writing.** Choose three questions to discuss with a partner. Write the rest, looking back at the story, or using your own words.

1. What are some of the reasons for the Apollo Project?

_____

_____

_____

2. Why does it take so much time and money to develop all the things necessary for the trip to the moon?

_____

_____

_____

3. How do Armstrong and Aldrin leave the spaceship to land on the moon?

_____

_____

_____

4. What do Armstrong's words mean when he says, "That's one small step for a man, and one giant leap for mankind"?

_____

_____

_____

5. Is it likely that the flag they place on the moon is still there? Why?

_____

_____

_____

B. Choose the best endings for these sentences.

1. Space exploration is important because

   a. people's desire to fly is as old as history.
   b. President Kennedy wants to keep his promise to land a man on the moon.
   c. scientists need to understand the universe.

2. The astronauts need special space suits because

   a. they need to keep their body temperatures normal.
   b. there is no air or water or weather on the moon.
   c. they cannot live or breathe on the moon without these suits.

3. The first person to walk in space is

   a. Neil Armstrong
   b. Edwin Aldrin
   c. Alexei Leonov

Chapter Fourteen, Overview

A Time of Anger

During the 1960's and early 70's the U.S. and the Soviet Union continue the Cold War. At the same time, another kind of struggle is going on inside the United States. It is the bitter struggle of black people, American Indians, Mexican Americans and women to make the promise of America come true for them. They want equal justice, equal opportunity, and they want it now.

Night after night, the American people see this great struggle on their television screens. They see black children trying to enter all-white Southern schools while angry white people threaten them. They see Freedom Riders, mostly college students, coming to the South in buses to encourage blacks to vote.

They see American Indians seize¹ Alcatraz Island, in San Francisco Bay, to show that they are able to fight for their rights. Indians, or Native Americans as they call themselves, have less money, less education and less opportunity as a group than others in America.

The American people see Mexican American farm workers, led by Caesar Chavez, going on strike for better working conditions. They, too, organize to vote so that they can begin to have political power.

Women are also marching, demanding equal pay for equal work. They are no longer willing to accept less money for doing the same job as men. They are fighting for their rights, and some believe that these include whether or not to have children.

While all this is going on at home, the United States is getting deeper and deeper into the war in Vietnam.

Vietnam is a French colony. After World War II, the Vietnamese people fight for and win their independence from France. Until there can be an election, Vietnam is divided into two parts, North and South. China and the Soviet Union support the communist government of North Vietnam. The United States helps to set up an independent government in South Vietnam, which it supports with arms and money. Soon North and South Vietnam are at war. At first, America sends only a few soldiers to fight in Vietnam. Then it sends more and more. By the time Lyndon B. Johnson becomes president, after the death of Kennedy, there are 100,000 Americans fighting in Vietnam. All this is happening without a declaration of war by congress, which the constitution requires.

In the United States, the Vietnam War becomes less popular from day to day. Finally, there is so much anger in the country about this war that Lyndon Johnson feels unable to accept the Democratic Party's nomination for a second term.

Richard M. Nixon becomes the next president in 1968. He takes some important steps toward ending the Cold War. He accepts an invitation to visit Communist China. After this successful visit, he encourages trade between China and the United States. He also makes good progress in talks with the Soviet Union.

But the problem of the war in Vietnam goes on. There are now half a million United States soldiers fighting there. Almost every night of the week television shows the bodies of American sons arriving home to be buried.

Anger grows in the colleges and universities. Students organize a march. Three hundred thousand come to Washington, many of them shouting, "Hell no, we won't go!" They do not believe in the war, and they are not going to fight in Vietnam.

---

[1] **seize** — take by force

Chapter Fourteen, Overview
A Time of Anger

Exercises

A. **Reading Comprehension — Discussion and Writing.** Choose three questions to discuss with a partner. Write the rest, looking back at the story, or using your own words.

   1. What groups of people are struggling in the United States in the 1960's and 1970's?

   _____

   _____

   _____

   2. How do these groups fight for what they want?

   _____

   _____

   _____

   3. Why are North and South Vietnam divided at the time they become independent from France?

   _____

   _____

   _____

   4. What are some of the reasons the Vietnam War is unpopular in the United States?

   _____

   _____

   _____

5. What does Richard Nixon do to help end the Cold War in China?

_____

_____

_____

B. Choose the best answer for each sentence.

1. At this time many people are struggling for

   a. political power.
   b. segregated schools.
   c. equal work.

2. The United States

   a. divides Vietnam into two parts.
   b. sends South Vietnam arms, money and soldiers.
   c. sets up an independent government in North Vietnam.

3. American people at home see

   a. many groups getting equal justice and equal opportunity they want.
   b. the election in Vietnam.
   c. the bodies of Americans arriving home to be buried.

Chapter Fourteen, Story One

We Shall Overcome

Black Americans win their freedom from slavery in 1865. But freedom does not give them justice. It does not give them opportunity. They live in poor, segregated[2] neighborhoods. Their children attend segregated schools. In the South, they are kept from registering to vote, and must obey local rules that they sit at the back of buses they ride.

In 1955, in Montgomery, Alabama, a quiet, black woman decides that she has had enough. Her name is Rosa Parks. At this time, she's not a famous person, she's not anybody important. She is just a hard-working woman whose feet hurt. One night, as she is riding home from work, the bus driver tells Mrs. Parks to give up her seat and go stand in the back of the bus so a white man can sit down. She finds the courage to refuse, and when she does the police arrest her and take her to jail.

The black community of Montgomery unites in support of Rosa Parks. They boycott[3] the Montgomery buses. For 381 difficult days almost every black person in

Wide World Photos

Martin Luther King

Montgomery walks to work or school. The Montgomery bus boycott begins to appear often on the television news. One of its young organizers, Dr. Martin Luther King, Jr., soon becomes a familiar face to most Americans.

Dr. King, a Baptist minister, does not believe in violence.

"Don't ever let anyone pull you so low as to hate them," he teaches. He always reminds his followers to protest[4] peacefully. When whites attack them, even when someone throws a bomb into Dr. King's home, the black people of the Montgomery boycott answer white violence with freedom songs.

"We shall overcome," they sing,
"We shall overcome.
"For deep in my heart, I do believe
"We shall overcome some day."

In 1956, the Supreme Court says that bus segregation in Montgomery is illegal. This helps blacks to fight segregation in other Southern cities. It is a victory, but there is still a long road to justice and equality.

Martin Luther King continues to teach and practice non-violence. In 1964, he wins the Nobel Prize[5] for peace, a very great honor for this important black leader. Four years later King is murdered, and black anger explodes. Terrible violence, so long under tight control, breaks out in many large cities. Night after night there is burning, fighting and shooting. Before it is over, forty-six people die, thousands are hurt, and millions of dollars worth of property is destroyed.

This is a time of anger in America.

[1] **segregated** — separate from the main body
[2] **boycott** — refuse to buy, sell or use something
[3] **protest** — show disapproval strongly
[4] **Nobel Prize** — a yearly prize given for great work in the sciences, in arts, and in peace

★ ★

Chapter Fourteen, Story One

Exercises

A. **Reading Comprehension — Discussion and Writing.** Choose four questions to discuss with a partner. Write the rest, looking back at the story, or using your own words.

1. How does segregation affect the lives of black Americans in the South in 1955?

_____

_____

_____

2. What happens to Rosa Parks as she rides on the bus in Montgomery, Alabama?

_____

_____

_____

3. How does the black community of Alabama support Rosa Parks?

_____

_____

_____

4. What kind of protest does Dr. Martin Luther King teach his followers?

_____

_____

_____

5. What is the Supreme Court's decision in November, 1956, and what effect does it have in other cities?

_____

_____

_____

6. What great honor does Dr. King receive in 1964?

_____

_____

_____

7. What happens when Dr. King is murdered?

_____

_____

_____

B. **True or False?** Circle true or false. Find information in the story to support your answer.

1. True or false? After black Americans become free from slavery in 1865, they find justice and opportunity in America.

_____

_____

2. True or false? When the bus driver tells her to go to the back of the bus, Rosa Parks does not have the courage to refuse.

_____

_____

3. True or false? The black community organizes a boycott against the Montgomery bus company.

_____

_____

4. True or false? Dr. King tells his people not to hate, and not to fight.

_____

_____

Chapter Fourteen, Story Two

Kent State University

One of the reasons Richard M. Nixon is elected president is that he promises he is going to get the United States out of Vietnam. This war is becoming more and more unpopular with the American people.

Weeks and months pass. The war continues. The number of Vietnamese and American people killed rises every day. Students are especially disappointed with their government for not ending the war. They show their anger in the way young people do: loudly, sometimes wildly.

On April 30, 1970, President Nixon goes on TV to tell the world that American forces are invading Cambodia, a small country next to Vietnam, where Vietnamese troops are hiding. Many United States citizens protest, and an angry congress decides that Nixon may not use American forces without its approval. The invasion fails, but the United States continues to supply bombs that explode over Laos, Cambodia and Vietnam. It seems to many people that, instead of ending, the war is getting worse.

At Kent State University, in Ohio, there is bitter feeling against the government. Some of the students set fire to one of the university buildings. Nobody is hurt, but the next morning three hundred National Guards arrive. Their commanding officer says, "These students are going to have to find out what law and order is all about."

On the morning of May 4, 1970, the students at Kent State find out. When the 10:45 classes end, about six hundred students hold a peaceful meeting. The student speakers criticize the president for bombing Cambodia. Suddenly, a university police officer orders the meeting to come to an end. When the students do not leave at once, the National Guards, wearing gas masks, use tear gas against the young people. Then they shoot into the crowd. Four young men and women fall dead. Nine others are seriously injured.

The shooting at Kent State shocks the nation. Ten days later, two black students who are also demonstrating against the war are killed at Jackson State College in Mississippi. Anger and violence spread through most American colleges and universities. In 1970 alone, more than seven thousand students are arrested while they are protesting against the war.

Richard Nixon does not want to go down in history as the first American president to lose a war. He tells the public that he is not concerned by all the protest. He even plans to increase military action. But years later, he writes that it is the power of public opinion that finally makes him drop his plans.

Richard M. Nixon, Inaugural Address, 1/20/69

Chapter Fourteen, Story Two
Kent State University

Exercises

A. **Reading Comprehension — Discussion and Writing.** Choose two questions to discuss with a partner. Write the rest, looking back at the story, or using your own words.

1. How do students and other United States citizens react to the continuing war in 1970?

2. What does congress decide on April 30, 1970?

3. How do the police and National Guard react to student protests at Kent State University and Jackson College?

4. What does President Nixon think about the power of public opinion?

B. Choose the best answer for these sentences.

1. In the 1970's, students sometimes show their anger against the war

   a. with demonstrations against the National Guard.
   b. with violent protests.
   c. by throwing tear gas.

2. In 1970,

   a. the war seems to be ending.
   b. the war seems to be continuing.
   c. the congress decides to end the war.

3. During this period, President Nixon tells the people he

   a. is ending the war in Vietnam.
   b. is authorizing supplies of war material against Laos, Cambodia and Vietnam.
   c. is the first president to lose a war.

Chapter Fifteen

From There to Here, From Then to Now

The years of protest and anger come slowly to an end. South Vietnam loses the war. The United States has to pull out, but at least it is over.

Soon, South Vietnamese begin leaving their country. They are not safe from the government that takes power there. They and many thousands of people from other countries come to the United States in the 1970's and 1980's and 1990's. They come from El Salvador, Guatemala, Mexico, Cuba, Samoa, Taiwan, Thailand, Ethiopia, Lebanon, Cambodia and many other places to escape from hunger, war, or both. They become the new Americans, the new Pilgrims.

In 1974, Richard M. Nixon becomes the first American President to resign, to give up his position, and return to private life. People working for him confess to illegal activities in a Washington D.C. building named Watergate. For months, the Watergate story, as it is called, is the biggest thing on television and in the newspapers. Nixon resigns because Congress threatens to impeach him.

Gerald Ford, the Vice-President, finishes Nixon's unfinished term in the White House. He gives Richard Nixon a pardon. Now Nixon cannot be tried in court for any crimes related to Watergate. After Ford, Jimmy Carter is elected President. He serves only four years. Ronald Reagan easily defeats Carter in the Presidential election of 1980. Reagan becomes one of the most popular Presidents in recent times. During the eight years President Reagan is in the White House, Americans begin to feel better about themselves and their country.

There are many things to feel better about. For the first time, a woman, Sandra Day O'Connor, becomes one of the nine judges of the United States Supreme Court. Another woman, Geraldine Ferraro, receives the Democratic party's nomination for Vice-President. Her party loses the election, but the fact that a woman, after two hundred years, is at last nominated for such a high office is important to the women of America.

For black Americans, there are some continuing success stories. Perhaps one of the most important black Americans is Thurgood Marshall, who continues to serve on the Supreme Court for more than twenty years until he retires in 1991. As a judge, he does more than almost anyone else to defeat segregation — in the Court, where it counts.

Through these years, minorities — the small, less powerful groups — continue their fight for civil rights. Among them are black Americans, Native Americans, Hispanics, Asians and women. All are asking for better treatment and opportunities. They are asking for their share of the American dream.

The black protest movement, using non-violent resistance, powerful speech and boycotts, wins reforms for blacks. Other minority groups follow the black model and also make legal gains. Mexican farm laborers in California work long hours under terrible working conditions for very little pay. Cesar Chavez, a Mexican American born in Arizona, organizes the Farm Workers Union. When they go on strike against the grape industry, he persuades many people all over the country to boycott grapes. In 1975, he succeeds in getting laws passed to improve conditions for those workers.

There are some things to feel bad about, too. The national debt, the amount of money the United States owes, is larger than at any time in history. Once a lender nation, the United States is now a borrower nation and has to borrow money from other, richer countries like Japan.

A new disease, AIDS, for which there is no cure, threatens to infect almost fifteen million Americans by the end of the twentieth century.

The earth itself may be in danger from the very progress that science makes. Some scientists believe that harmful gases from automobiles and industry are causing the temperature of the earth to rise. This is known as the greenhouse effect. The oceans, rivers, and forests of the world are also in danger and must be protected.

Great improvements and changes in life come from new technology. In medicine, doctors can now replace worn-out hearts and other organs of the body. People can live longer, healthier lives. For business and industry, machines can do the work of people. Computers make information available to everyone, instantly.

Sadly, all these improvements do not change the fact that one out of five American children is poor. In the 1980s and 1990s rich families get richer, and poor families get a little poorer. In every city there are homeless people sleeping under bridges, in subway stations, wherever they can keep warm.

In 1988, for the first time in American history, a black, Jesse Jackson, is a serious candidate for president of the United States.

Another success occurs in January, 1990. Lawrence D. Wilder, the grandson of slaves, becomes governor of the state of Virginia. He is the first black elected governor in United States history.

Republican George Bush is elected president in 1988. He struggles with some of the problems left over from the Reagan years. One major problem is Nicaragua, in Central America. The United States is against the revolutionary government, which the Soviet Union and Cuba support. An election in Nicaragua brings peace to that war-torn country. During President Reagan's final year and President Bush's first year in office, the countries of Eastern Europe, under the leadership of Mikhail Gorbachev, seem to be slowly moving toward democracy. Then, about the end of 1989, the Soviet

Union begins to fall apart and now no longer exists as a great world power. Some former Soviet republics break away and become independent states. Boris Yeltsin replaces Gorbachev. He rapidly pushes Russia, as the most important of the former Soviet Republics is once again called, toward becoming a capitalist society. This is a welcome event for the United States, but it produces many new problems. The breakup of the Soviet Union and the former Yugoslavia results in terrible wars between people of different religious and ethnic backgrounds. In the United States, because there is no longer a mighty enemy against whom to arm, American industry slows down. Millions of jobs are lost. Money for schools, hospitals, social services becomes harder to get. And still the national debt grows. As the presidential election of 1992 approaches, George Bush loses popularity. There is great dissatisfaction with government at all levels.

After twelve years of Republican presidents, a Democrat, Bill Clinton, Governor of Arkansas, wins the 1992 election, but by very few votes. He promises economic and social programs to improve the lives of all Americans. He promises to cooperate with world leaders to improve economic conditions worldwide. He brings more women into important positions in government, including Madeleine Albright, the first woman Secretary of State.

Acts of violence and terrorism that are common in other parts of the world come to the United States. The tallest building in New York, the World Trade Center, is bombed. In 1994, the Federal Building in Oklahoma City is also bombed with great loss of life. In the elections of 1994, enough Republicans are able to defeat Democrats to get control of both houses of Congress. But employment is high, business is good, and by the time of the 1996 presidential election most U.S. citizens are very pleased with their lives. Bill Clinton is re-elected by a huge majority.

The Democratic president and the Republican Congress struggle but finally agree on a balanced budget for the first time in more than twenty years. Most new laws take power away from government and end its responsibility to help minorities, immigrants, the arts, women and poor people.

There are still no answers for many of these problems. Americans can be proud of the good things their country does and sorry for its mistakes. There is a saying, "Those who do not learn from history may have to repeat it." How well do Americans understand the lessons of history? We do not know yet. In a world of increasingly difficult social and economic problems, Americans need to hold on to the best values from their past.

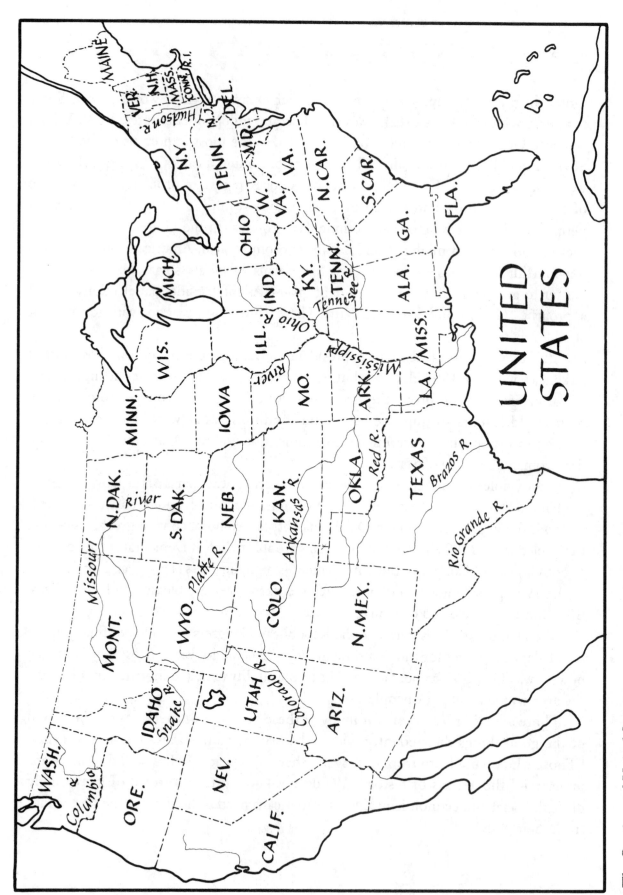

UNITED STATES

The Continental United States

Answer Key

Chapter 1, Overview, THE EXPLORERS

B. VOCABULARY
1. fears
2. adventures
3. spices
4. explores

C. DEFINITIONS
1. d
2. e
3. a
4. c
5. b

Chapter 1, CHRISTOPHER COLUMBUS (Part 1)

B. VOCABULARY
1. sailor
2. ambitious
3. 3,000 miles
4. Grand Admiral of the Ocean Sea
5. important

C. DEFINITIONS
1. ambitious
2. support
3. authority

Chapter 1, CHRISTOPHER COLUMBUS (Part 2)

B. VOCABULARY
1. frighten
2. coast
3. hero's
4. chains
5. discoverer

C. DEFINITIONS
1. fears
2. popular

Chapter 2, Overview, COMING TO AMERICA

B. VOCABULARY
1. religion, establishes
2. treasure, master
3. settlements, freedom

C. DEFINITIONS
1. population
2. world power
3. Pilgrims
4. against their will
5. willingly

Chapter 2, Story 1, THE FIRST THANKSGIVING

A. READING COMPREHENSION
1. True. As the years pass, some Puritans become unhappy with other Protestant churches. OR One group of Puritans, hoping to find religious freedom, decides to leave England and go to Virginia.
2. False. The Mayflower lands off the coast of what is later to be the colony of Massachusetts.
3. False. Everyone lives in fear of an attack by Indians, but it doesn't happen.
4. False. The peace between the Pilgrims and the Indians lasts only fifty years.

B. VOCABULARY
1. Puritans, Roman, Catholic, influence
2. religious
3. colony
4. voyage
5. dead, secretly, few
6. Thanksgiving

C. FILL IN THE BLANKS
1. Puritans
2. freedom
3. New World
4. Pilgrims
5. voyage
6. death
7. attack

8. teach
9. Mayflower
10. themselves
11. deer
12. games
13. intend

Chapter 2, Story 2, ROGER WILLIAMS

B. VOCABULARY
1. a. Puritans
2. b. church, c. state
3. d. belongs, e. Indians
4. f. popular

Chapter 3, Overview, STORM CLOUDS OVER THE COLONIES

B. VOCABULARY
1. Great Britain
2. govern
3. members
4. obey

C. DEFINITIONS
1. self-government
2. taxes
3. representation

Chapter 3, Story 1, THE BOSTON MASSACRE

B. VOCABULARY
1. insults
2. unpleasant
3. represent
4. justice

C. DEFINITIONS
1. b
2. c
3. a
4. d

Chapter 3, Story 2, THE BOSTON TEA PARTY

B. VOCABULARY
1. collect taxes
2. political leaders
3. Indians, feathers, Boston Tea Party

4. obey, uniting

C. DEFINITIONS
1. intends
2. popular
3. refuses to allow

Chapter 3, Story 3, THE MIDNIGHT RIDE OF PAUL REVERE

B. VOCABULARY
1. defend
2. arranges
3. warning
4. unexpected

C. DEFINITIONS
1. b
2. d
3. a
4. c
5. e

Chapter 4, Overview, BIRTH OF A NATION

B. VOCABULARY
1. separating
2. training, uniforms, gun powder
3. immigrant

C. CLASS DISCUSSION

Chapter 4, Story 1, THE DECLARATION OF INDEPENDENCE

B. VOCABULARY
1. e
2. c
3. b
4. a
5. d

C. DEFINITIONS
1. intend
2. fails
3. compromise

Chapter 4, Story 2, WASHINGTON AT VALLEY FORGE

B. VOCABULARY
1. reputation
2. Philadelphia, food, clothing
3. France, Spain, Holland

C. DEFINITIONS
For class discussion

Chapter 4, Story 3, THE CONSTITUTION

B. VOCABULARY
1. peace agreement, laws, constitution, money
2. central, federal, states' rights
3. unite

C. DEFINITIONS
1. document
2. compromises
3. nation
4. Bill of Rights

Chapter 5, Overview, GOING WEST

B. TRUE OR FALSE
1. False. In 1803, France sells the United States a very large piece of land. It is known as the Louisiana Purchase.
2. False. They hope to frighten away Indians who might attack.
3. True. "For as long as the sun shines or the waters run in the rivers."
4. False. One after another the agreements are broken.
5. True. The history of the American Indian is a history of broken promises.

C. VOCABULARY
1. grasslands
2. honor, pity
3. power
4. newcomers

Chapter 5, Story 1, THE TRAIL OF TEARS

B. CHOOSING THE BEST ANSWER
1. c

2. b
3. a

C. DEFINITIONS
1. b
2. e
3. d
4. a
5. c

Chapter 5, Story 2, THE FORTY-NINERS

B. CHOOSING THE BEST ANSWER
1. c
2. a

Chapter 6, Overview, SLAVERY

B. TRUE OR FALSE
1. False. In the North, there are many factories, but most farms are small.
2. False. This law says that any new state may vote to decide whether or not to allow slavery.
3. True. These people are called abolitionists because they want to abolish, or put an end to slavery.
4. False. The Court says a slave is a property, not a citizen, and slave owners have the right to take their property anywhere they wish.

C. VOCABULARY
1. a. cotton, b. seed
2. c. suffering, d. abolition

Chapter 6, Story 1, HARRIET TUBMAN AND THE UNDERGROUND RAILROAD

B. VOCABULARY
a. conductors
b. stations
c. reward

Chapter 6, Story 2, JOHN BROWN AT HARPER'S FERRY

B. VOCABULARY
1. a. escaping, b. secret, c. room
2. a. revenge, b. abolitionists

3. a. federal, b. government
4. a. guns, b. prisoners
5. a. murder, b. treason
6. a. criminal, b. hero, c. martyr

Chapter 7, Overview, THE CIVIL WAR

B. CHOOSING THE BEST ANSWER
1.c
2.b
3.b
4.a

C. COMPLETE THE SENTENCES
1. b
2. e
3. c
4. d
5. a

Chapter 7, Story, ABRAHAM LINCOLN (Part 1)

B. VOCABULARY
1. slave
2. clear
3. political
4. law
5. son-in-law
6. Mexican War

Chapter 7, Story, ABRAHAM LINCOLN (Part 2)

B. TRUE OR FALSE
1. True. Stephen A. Douglas, now a powerful U.S. senator, supports the Kansas Nebraska Act of 1854.
2. True. Republicans oppose slavery for the new territories.
3. True. Abraham Lincoln, the sixteenth president of the United States, takes his wife and children to Washington D.C. The Civil War begins soon after.
4. False. He promises that the world will never forget these soldiers who died to give the country "a new birth of freedom."
5. False. He allows them to return home.
6. False. They return to their farms to work

and to reconstruct their lives and their cities. It is a sad victory.

Chapter 8, Overview, THE AGE OF INDUSTRY AND INVENTION

B. DEFINITIONS
1. d
2. a
3. b
4. e
5. c

Chapter 8, Story 1, MR. SINGER'S SEWING MACHINE

B. TRUE OR FALSE
1. False. In 1851 there are at least half a dozen men who claim that they are inventors of the sewing machine.
2. False. He wants to be an actor.
3. False. All this time, Singer is making and selling his sewing machines just as fast as he can.
4. True. Many other businesses begin to use the installment plan to make it easier to sell their products.
5. False. It takes millions of them out of the home, off the farm, and into industry.
6. True. He is now a very, very wealthy man, and he builds himself a house in France.

Chapter 8, Story 2, THE WRIGHT BROTHERS AND THEIR FLYING MACHINE

B. VOCABULARY
1. a. scientists, b. engineers
2. c. experiments, d. observation
3. e. biplane
4. f. claim
5. g. war, h. machine
6. i. flight

Chapter 9, Overview, THE LAND OF OPPORTUNITY

B. CHOOSING THE BEST ANSWER
1. a, b, c, all are correct

2. a
3. c
4. a

Chapter 9, Story 1, STATUE OF LIBERTY

B. COMPLETE THE SENTENCES
1. d
2. a
3. b
4. e
5. c

Chapter 9, Story 2, THE CHINESE IN CALIFORNIA

B. COMPLETE THE SENTENCES
1. don't want to share the gold with these strange looking men.
2. they go on strike
3. nine thousand are Chinese.
4. for every one Chinese woman in the United States.

Chapter 10, Overview, OVER THERE (Part 1)

B. CHOOSING THE BEST ANSWER
1. c
2. b
3. a

Chapter 10, OVER THERE (Part 2)

B. CHOOSING THE BEST ANSWER
1. c
2. a
3. c

Chapter 10, WOODROW WILSON and the War to End All Wars (Part 1)

B.
No questions

Chapter 10, WOODROW WILSON and the War to End All Wars (Part 2)

B. TRUE OR FALSE
1. True. They also include a League of Nations, a kind of world congress.
2. False. Wilson hopes for "peace without victory."
3. False. The Republican congress does not intend to support either the peace treaty or the League of Nations.
4. True. America must support the Versailles Treaty and the League of Nations, he tells the citizens.
5. True. Without support from the powerful United States, the League is not able to keep the peace.

Chapter 11, Overview, THE GREAT DEPRESSION

B. CHOOSING THE CORRECT ENDING
1. b
2. c
3. b

Chapter 11, Story 1, THE DUST BOWL

B. VOCABULARY
1. blows, fiery
2. season
3. fall, fail
4. growers
5. crops
6. use
7. possessions

Chapter 11, Story 2, F.D.R.

B. CHOOSING THE CORRECT ENDING
1. c
2. a
3. c
4. b

Chapter 12, Overview, WORLD WAR II (Part 1)

B. VOCABULARY
1. persuades, blame
2. Europe, democracy
3. peace treaty

C. DEFINITIONS
For class discussion

Chapter 12, Overview, WORLD WAR II (Part 2)

B. VOCABULARY
1. radio, surrender
2. iron, oil
3. invasion
4. surprise attack
5. military loss

C. DEFINITIONS
1. e
2. c
3. d
4. a
5. b

Chapter 12, Story 1, VICTORY IN EUROPE

B. VOCABULARY
1. north, east
2. Berlin
3. surrenders

C. DEFINITIONS
1. invade
2. defeat
3. secret hiding place

Chapter 12, Story 2, VICTORY IN JAPAN

B. VOCABULARY
1. frightening, continue
2. surrender
3. effects

C. DEFINITIONS
For class discussion

Chapter 13, Overview, THE COLD WAR

B. TRUE OR FALSE
1. True. Now the United States is not the only country able to destroy the world.
2. True. They decide it is the fault of American schools for not teaching as much mathematics or science as the Russians do.
3. False. Congress allows twenty billion dollars to fund Project Apollo.

Chapter 13, Story 1, JOHN FITZGERALD KENNEDY

B. TRUE OR FALSE
1. True. All his sisters and brothers and their husbands and wives work hard for his election.
2. True. The Soviet Union supports Castro and supplies war materials.
3. False. Cubans, who are against Castro, are led by some American officers.
4. True. It is a grand moment in the non-violent civil rights movement.

Chapter 13, Story 2, APOLLO 11 GOES TO THE MOON

B. CHOOSING THE BEST ENDINGS
1. c
2. a, b, c, all are correct
3. c

Chapter 14, Overview, A TIME OF ANGER

B. CHOOSING THE BEST ANSWER
1. a
2. b
3. c

Chapter 14, Story 1, WE SHALL OVERCOME

B. TRUE OR FALSE
1. False. Freedom does not give them justice. It does not give them opportunity.
2. False. She finds the courage to refuse.
3. True. They boycott the Montgomery buses.
4. True. Martin Luther King continues to teach and practice non-violence.

Chapter 14, Story 2, KENT STATE

B. CHOOSING THE BEST ANSWER
1. b
2. b
3. b